MW00885272

Numerology for Beginners

Numerology Foundations - Secret Meaning of the Numbers in Your Life - Insight and Guidance Toward Life Mastery

Clarissa Lightheart

Disclaimer and Copyrights

All rights reserved 2017 © Clarissa Lightheart and Maplewood Publishing. No part of this publication or the information in it may be quoted from or reproduced in any form by means such as printing, scanning, photocopying, or otherwise without prior written permission of the copyright holder.

Disclaimer and Terms of Use: Effort has been made to ensure that the information in this book is accurate and complete. However, the author and the publisher do not warrant the accuracy of the information, text, and graphics contained within the book due to the rapidly changing nature of science, research, known and unknown facts, and internet. The author and the publisher do not hold any responsibility for errors, omissions, or contrary interpretation of the subject matter herein. This book is presented solely for motivational and informational purposes only.

ISBN: 978-1979055895

Printed in the United States

MAPLEWOOD
— PUBLISHING —

Avant-Propos

Have you ever wondered if there is a way to connect science and spirituality? If there is something tangible and logical about metaphysics? Many people ask these questions on their path to self-discovery, and what you are about to discover is that the answer is yes—through the science of numerology.

Numerology is like a guide book for putting together the puzzle of your life. The science of numerology was discovered thousands of years ago, and its concepts have been proven time and time again: Numbers carry their own energies, and their vibrations affect our lives both directly and indirectly. The first time you look at a numerology chart, chances are you will be overwhelmed. There are so many numbers that it seems that only the truly gifted could properly interpret it. The truth is that understanding numerology is easy and within the grasp of anyone who is interested in learning both the art and the science.

This book breaks numerology down into easy-to-understand parts. It will guide you through calculating your own numerical influences and understanding how they affect your life. Understanding numerology might not change the path that you are on, but it will help you discover how to more fully understand and grow from it, and that is what each of us is here for.

Contents

Introduction to Numerology..1
Developing Your Intuitive Power...5
   Eight Activities to Develop and Strengthen Your Intuition 7
Reincarnation and Karmic Influence....................................11
The 5 Core Numbers of Numerology Readings 16
   Life Path Numbers...18
   Destiny Numbers..21
   Soul Numbers 25
   Personality Numbers 29
   Birth Day Number...33
Life Cycles: Personal Years, Essence Numbers and Pinnacle
Cycles 35
   Personal Years and the Nine-Year Cycle of Change.........35
   Essence Numbers 42
   Pinnacle Cycles 50
Pythagorean Arrows: Lines of Individuality and Circles of
Frustration 59
Connecting the Past, Present and Future: Karmic Debt and
Karmic Lessons 65
   Karmic Debt 66
   Karmic Lesson Numbers 72
The Meaning of the Numbers..75
   Numbers One through Nine: The Foundation of
   Numerology 75
   The Masters: 11, 22 and 33..126
Living Consciously Through Numerology 131
Also by Clarissa Lightheart 135

Introduction to Numerology

Have you ever wandered through life wishing that there was a magical tool that could help you figure out some pieces of the puzzle? Some like to believe that no such magical tool exists. I, on the other hand, believe that it does exist, except that its roots lie far more in science than magic. I am, of course, referring to numerology.

Numerology is the science of numbers and their energies. Each number has a unique energy connected to it, and when and how these numbers appear in your life can give you great insight into your physical, emotional and spiritual self. As we learn to read the energy associated with numbers, we learn that they tell us a story that provides us with insight and clarity into the physical, emotional and spiritual aspects of our lives. This is the art and science of numerology, and it all started many, many years ago with a man named Pythagoras.

Pythagoras of Samos was born in the year 560 B.C. and became a renowned philosopher and religious leader. However, it was his mathematical genius on which his legacy would be built. When Pythagoras was in his thirties, he founded his own university in the Grecian colony of Crotona in southern Italy. This is where the philosophy and science of numerology was born.

While Pythagoras had a very open-door policy about whom he would accept into his university, he was strict about his students being devoted and committed to their studies. Of the major teachings at his university, the main one was a three-part course in personal self-development. The three components were labeled "Preparation," "Purification" and "Perfection," and each one centered on mathematical concepts and the energies of numbers.

What many people don't realize is that numerology is not strictly an intuitive art. It is intuition combined with mathematics and science. If you have ever taken a geometry class, then you probably already recognize the name Pythagoras as the mind behind the Pythagorean Theorem, which states that for right triangles, the sum of the squares of each of the adjacent sides will equal the square of the hypotenuse. (For those who are not mathematically inclined, I don't blame you for skipping over that last bit; however, I feel that it is important to note that the same man who formulated the underlying principles of numerology was and still is a highly respected mathematician.)

According to Pythagoras, every planet has a sound, or vibration, that is unique to itself. Pythagoras could connect specific numbers to these planetary vibrations, and in the act of doing so, assigned specific traits and energies to each of the numbers. From there, he assigned alphabetical symbols to each number— and there you have the birth of numerology, a combination of spirituality, mathematics and astronomy.

Today, we use numerology to gain insights into our inner selves and to help guide us through the lessons and challenges of each incarnation. The spirit, or the soul, is a work in progress, and with each part of the journey, there will be certain numbers and energies that have a significant influence on the process.

I like to point out that there is a scientific basis to numerology, because I feel that it helps take away some of the air of mysticism that surrounds it. Some people like this air of mysticism, but others can be quick to dismiss anything mystical as being unsubstantiated. Taking the time to point out the scientific and mathematical roots makes numerology more substantial in the more cynical of minds. That said, numerology is equal parts science and intuition. Without intuition, and an

2

understanding of each of the numbers, it is nearly impossible to apply the energies of the numbers to your life.

For that reason, I am starting off this book by talking a little bit about intuition and how to develop it. From there, we will explore the many different aspects of numerology. With practice, patience and openness, you will soon be able to calculate basic charts for yourself and others, and be able to interpret them with thoughtful skill and ease. Numerology can enrich and enhance your journey in this life by providing you with insight and guidance. In essence, numerology is like a lifelong best friend— except the numbers tell secrets about yourself that you may not even be aware of yet.

Developing Your Intuitive Power

While numerology is considered a metaphysical practice by many, it isn't exactly the same in terms of being an intuitive art as some of the other metaphysical arts, many of which rely heavily upon intuition. You might look at numerology, with its solid foundation of mathematical numbers, and think that intuition does not play a very big part. While it is true that you can simply read this book, determine your numbers and memorize the descriptions, you aren't really doing yourself any service by not looking inward and further analyzing the energy of the numbers. For this, a bit of intuition comes in handy.

Intuition is not a skill that is reserved only for those with the gift of divination. In fact, intuition is something that is innate in all of us. Each and every one of us possesses it, and it is considered to be a real, legitimate phenomenon. Research has shown that our brains are capable of picking up on patterns in life and then analyzing and responding to them in a fraction of a second. Let's stop for a minute and consider what patterns are. If the first thing that came to your mind was numerical configurations, then you are correct. Patterns are numbers, even when they don't have anything obvious to do with mathematics. Even the most seemingly chaotic or chance occurrences are numerical in nature. In fact, a great deal of math and science research has been devoted to such topics. It makes perfect sense that we can attune ourselves to these patterns in the form of intuition.

At the most basic level, intuition is a function of our brains storing, processing and retrieving the information that is received on a subconscious level. Your subconscious can be viewed as a bridge between your physical self and your higher self. It is along this bridge that information and insight travel. This provides us with that inner voice, the natural sense of knowing and recognition. Scientifically, the power of intuition is substantial, and we have only begun to harness its true potential.

So, how can developing intuition assist you with numerology? The descriptions in this book of the energies associated with each number are quite basic. In truth, a thorough examination of each could result in an entire book for each number, and even then, there would be subtleties that would be missing. This is because those subtleties can only be found within you. You might be able to memorize the energy description of each number, but you will benefit more if you are able to apply it to yourself or whoever you may be doing a numerology chart and reading for, and that takes intuition. A common mistake that many people make is to believe that they do not have good intuition, or any at all. First, intuition is something that we all have, but more importantly, there is no such thing as bad intuition. Maybe you have at some point felt as though your intuition led you astray, or caused you to seriously misjudge a person or situation. To this I believe there are two answers. The first is that perhaps you simply weren't tuned into your intuition and you let your conscious thought act as intuitive insight. My second thought on this is that although you may feel that your intuition was "wrong," there may have been a deeper, yet-to-be-discovered reason for your intuitive thoughts. Sometimes, rather than completely dismissing what you believe to be incorrect intuition, it is best to file it away, because chances are that at some point, it will all make sense to you.

Just like we all have intuition, we can all benefit from connecting to it on a more regular basis. Even those who feel that they have a strong connection with their intuition must use it regularly for it to remain strong. This has more to do with your ability to recognize and acknowledge your intuition than it does with your intuition becoming more powerful. Because the power of intuition depends heavily upon your ability to connect with it, it is a good idea to practice little daily rituals that help you to become more attuned to intuitive energy. These are not difficult activities; in fact, some of them will only take a few minutes of your time, while others simply require a little more awareness during your regular daily activities. To help you develop and strengthen your connection with your intuitive power, I have composed a list of eight simple activities. You can do one of these, or all of them. My advice is to do what feels best to you. If something feels too forced, it probably means that you are not ready or at a place where you would be open to the energy coming through that activity. So, set it aside and come back to it later, but only if you want to.

Eight Activities to Develop and Strengthen Your Intuition

1. Give validity to sudden feelings and changes in mood. Have you ever been out on a walk, peacefully enjoying nature, when suddenly you felt a little fearful? Or maybe you never play the lottery, but you had a sudden inclination to play and you ended up winning a little bit of extra money? It is important to pay extra-close attention to thoughts and feelings that catch you off guard or seem out of place. When these thoughts or changes in mood occur without warning or any idea where they came from, it is a sure sign that it is your intuition speaking to you.

2. Pay attention to the numbers that appear in your life, even the seemingly meaningless ones. Do you happen to look at the clock every afternoon at 1:37? Did you think you were going to be late, but actually arrived 2 minutes early? How did your meeting with 7 coworkers go? Sometimes the numbers in our daily lives are obvious, while other times it requires stopping to take notice. Make notes of the numbers that pop up in your everyday

activities and then go back and see how the energy of those numbers applies or how it affected the situation.

3. Write in a journal. It seems like journaling is the answer for everything, doesn't it? Want to eat better? Start a food journal. Want to sleep better? Start a journal to write down all the thoughts keeping you awake. Want to feel more gratitude? Write in a journal. I know it might seem overdone, but there is a reason that this is so. While you might not access all the "storage" space in your mind, it can be easy to be overwhelmed by all the little details when you try to keep track of them in your head. Writing things down signals to your brain that you have this information stored elsewhere. Besides, the act of physically writing something down and then rereading it will not only increase your memory of it, but also change your perspective. You might not notice all the sixes that have been appearing in your life until you go through your journal at the end of the week and see that the number has repeated over and over again. Write down everything that has to do with numbers and numerology, plus anything else that you feel the need to get down on paper. Those thoughts that come out of nowhere are your intuition, so make sure to honor it by writing them down too.

4. Give yourself ten minutes of quiet time every day. It can be difficult to tap into the power of your inner voice when you are constantly surrounded by noise. Many people like to have a few minutes of quiet, reflective or meditative thought early in the morning. I agree that this is a great way to start your day, but honestly it doesn't really matter what time of day you do it, as long as you make the commitment to yourself to have a few minutes of uninterrupted quiet time to be with your thoughts each day.

5. Practice daily numerology. Take note of the numerical energy that is attached to each individual day. You may notice that every day that is a two seems to go a certain way, or that you seem to have more difficulty on days with a specific number. Paying attention to these subtle changes in energy from day to day helps to develop your intuition.

6. Ask a question for which you don't have an answer. I don't mean go ask your best friend, but instead ask the universe, or your inner voice, for the answer to a question that you need help with, maybe something that you have been struggling with. Then, quietly wait for the answer. When it comes to you, make sure that you recognize it and respect it.

7. Go with your heart instead of your head. How many times have you felt one way about something, but then allowed yourself to overthink it and doubt your first inclination? Yes, some things deserve careful thought and consideration, but if you stop second guessing your first instinct you might be surprised to find that you already have many of the answers.

8. Test yourself. Do you doubt the power of your own intuition? Why not give it a test and see how it does. The next time you have an instinctual thought or are driven towards a certain action, go with it and see if your intuition leads you onto the right path. Remember that sometimes it takes a little while to see the end result or the big picture. Also, when testing the power of your intuition, make sure to pay attention to suggestion #7. Make sure that what you are testing is your actual intuition, and not your own conscious thought interfering.

Now that we have intuition covered, let's begin going more in depth about the different aspects of numerology.

Reincarnation and Karmic Influence

The theory behind reincarnation is that we are spiritual beings that are not bound to the confines of a singular physical life. Rather, as our time in one physical body ends, the soul is released, and when the time is appropriate, the soul re-enters a new physical body. Many spiritual and religious belief systems subscribe to the idea of reincarnation, although there are subtle differences in philosophy among them. Since reincarnation is so tightly connected to the practice of numerology, I feel it is important to give an introduction to the topic for those who are unfamiliar. However, it would take an entire book to go into the differences in philosophy regarding reincarnation among different theologies. For that reason, what you are about to read here is a simple overview. Your personal belief system made add more to this or be slightly different. The intent here is simply to illustrate how reincarnation and numerology are connected.

During the course of a typical life on the physical plane, we are born and then go through various stages of development from infancy through adulthood, until we reach old age. The average lifespan in the western world is about seventy-eight to eighty-two years. During this time, a typical person will accumulate many experiences and will have the opportunity to learn and grow spiritually as a person. For many people, the vision of leaving this life at peace with one's actions and development is ideal, although of course many of us miss the mark slightly. We can think of reincarnation as a mirror of this process. The soul is born and it enters a physical life. With each physical life, there are opportunities to grow and/or make mistakes. The idea is that with each life, we gain more experience and grow as a spiritual being until the soul becomes "old" and has fulfilled its destiny and become fully evolved. The journey through multiple lives is a learning and growing experience, much like the journey we are each experiencing in our present physical life. Some philosophies believe in an eternal wheel of reincarnation, where there is not necessarily progression from one life to the next. Many others believe that there is indeed a progression and that you never move backwards. You might become temporarily "stuck" as you work through some especially difficult issues, but you never actually regress. This is the theory that we subscribe to with numerology.

In numerology, there is a belief that you have influence over the direction your life will take. For example, the day that you choose to begin this life has a major influence in your numerology chart, as does the name that you were given at birth. In order for these influences to make sense, there is a need to accept that we personally chose to have these influences. You personally chose to have the life path number of 6 and the destiny number of 3, while also including the karma number of 14, for example. Your soul, on a spiritual level, understands what must be learned and experienced in this lifetime, and therefore sets out the numerological path to make that happen. This is how reincarnation is connected to numerology.

As I mentioned, the point is to experience and grow, and sometimes that means coming to terms with things that were not completed last time around. Karma comes from a Sanskrit word that means action. For every action that you make, there is a reaction. We can take this further and say that even our thoughts can have reactive consequences. When we do good, the reaction if usually positive. When we do wrong, the reaction is typically negative. When we do and think good or positive things, then the outcome is favorable and we can move on. On the other hand, when we do or think wrong or negative things, then the outcome causes hurt or an imbalance. These reactions cannot simply be left behind as we move forward. They must be accounted for and rectified. This is the action of Karma; taking accountability for our past wrongdoings, or lessons unlearned, and rectifying them in our current physical incarnation. You can choose not to address these karmic issues, but that does not mean that they go away. In fact, they will continue to stay attached to your soul until you are willing to face them and take the proper actions so that the energy can then be released into the universe. Like all energy, the energy that is connected to karmic issues is neither created nor destroyed; it is simply transferred is. The energy is there and will continue to stay with you until it can be released and recycled through the universe, where it comes back to you in the form of a positive response to your karmic resolution. You are the one who is in control of transforming the negative energy that surrounds you.

In numerology, there are two different ways that karma can appear in your chart: karmic debt and karmic lessons. Not everyone will have these numbers in their chart, but most people will have some type of karmic lesson that they are working through. A little later in this book I will help you determine if you have either of these numbers in your own chart. Karmic debt indicates that you committed some sort of wrongdoing or hurt in a previous life. It may have been the most recent incarnation before this one, or it could be something from further in the past that you have yet to work through. Karmic debt must be repaid for it to clear from your chart. Sometimes this karmic debt is owed to one person, but chances are that during that previous incarnation you chose to live a particular type of life, with a personality or tendencies that may have caused hurt or stress to multiple people. Therefore your karmic debt is more likely to be a generalized way of living in this life to rectify your way of life in the past.

I want to take a moment here and point out that having a karmic debt does not make you a bad person. Let's say you discover that you have a karmic debt number that corresponds to tendencies and personality traits that you strongly dislike in this life. It might be difficult for you to believe and accept that you were once that person. The truth is that you probably have such a strong aversion to that personality type because of your experience with it in the past. We are all here to learn and grow spiritually. In order to do that, we must pass through a variety of experiences, both positive and negative, and be on both the giving and receiving ends of each. Having a karmic debt does not mean that you are a bad person; it means that you are a spiritual being in the process of evolving. A telltale sign of an old soul is someone who demonstrates understanding, compassion and acceptance. These things come about through experience. You cannot naturally express these things without knowing, on a soul level, what it is like to be that person. Old souls have experienced being both good and "bad," they have experienced hardships and affluence, difficult lives and charmed ones, they have been incarnated in every color of skin, in every walk of life. This is the nature of the experience. Rather than feeling bad about your karmic debt, use it as an opportunity to grow past it.

The other karmic number that can show up in your numerology chart is that of karmic lessons. Unlike karmic debt, karmic lessons are not something that is "owed." Rather, they are lessons that should be accumulated throughout our lives. Having a karmic lesson is not a bad thing; in fact, it is quite positive. Karmic lessons can provide you with direction and a sense of purpose in this life. Think of karmic lessons as tools in a toolbox. A well-stocked toolbox will have every tool you might need for any situation. However, if you haven't yet acquired all your "tools," you might find that you don't have the right-sized socket for the job you are doing. You then must stop what you are doing, figure out how and where to find the right part, and then go through the actions of acquiring it. Once you have, you now have that part in your toolbox, so that next time you don't have to worry about it. Now, what if you could have a toolbox checklist that made it easy to identify what was in your toolbox and what was missing? This is similar to the purpose of recognizing your karmic lesson number(s).

Your karmic lesson number tells you what "tool" you are missing. You might look at it and think that you don't really need it, but it is on your list and unchecked for a reason, so you should strongly consider how to go about fulfilling the obligations associated with this number. Your karmic lesson number might be something that you have no interest in. In this case, you can benefit from some spiritual introspection to discover its importance in your life. On the other hand, you might be strongly connected to the energy of your karmic lesson and agree that it makes sense to focus on development in this area of your life.

When it comes to topics of reincarnation and karma, it is important to remember that inflated egos really have no place here. You shouldn't put too much thought or energy into who you were in a past incarnation. What matters now is that you are able to recognize your karmic debt or karmic lessons and grow from them. Remember that greatness in a past incarnation probably came with a cost, and you may be responsible for paying that cost now. Also, if you are one of the few who do not have any karmic debt or karmic lesson numbers in your chart, do not consider yourself better than others. It simply means that you agreed that you would not have any of these issues to work on in this life. You may have them in a future incarnation, or it could be that your "toolbox" is full and you have no debt from a previous incarnation. That does not mean that you are not at risk of incurring karmic debt in this life. You should also be mindful of not losing your "tools." You can't exactly move backwards in your soul's development, but that doesn't mean that you can act recklessly or with abandon, thinking that you have moved past the point of personal development. If you lose one of your "tools," rest assured that you will have to find it next time around.

The 5 Core Numbers of Numerology Readings

Numerology is the study of numbers and how they affect our lives. We know that each number has a vibrational energy associated with it, and we know that when these numbers show up in our lives, there is always something that we can learn or some insight that can be gained by attuning ourselves to the unique vibrational energy of each number. When you begin the study of numerology, it is appropriate to just get acquainted with each number and the energy that it represents. Over time, you might begin to notice these numbers showing up in your life in various ways, and you will begin to take notice of how they affect you. However, there are five specific numbers, which are unique to the individual, that really give us the greatest insight into the personality, ego and life path. We call these five numbers the "core" numbers of numerology, and they comprise the Life Path number, the Destiny number, the Soul number, the Personality number and the Birth Day number. To the person not attuned to these energies it might seem as though some of these core numbers overlap each other. They do, a little, but the subtle nuances between each of them are what really let us delve deeper into self-discovery along this life's journey.

As you read the description of the energy associated with each number a little later in this book, you will first be given a general overview of the number's energetic vibrations. Then I will break the number down further for you and provide a description of how each number acts when it is one of the five core numbers in your life.

If you have ever shied away from numerology because you thought the calculations were too complicated, I ask you to put away that notion. There is no magical secret formula that takes years of training to understand. All your numbers can be derived from either your birth day or your name, and from there, the only math involved is simple addition. As we discuss each type of core number, I will also illustrate for you how to easily find your own core number for that category.

I would also like to take a moment and talk about how these numbers are assigned to you and whether you are to carry the energy of these numbers with you through this life no matter what. There are certain numbers, like your life path number and birth day number, that absolutely will not change. After all, you cannot go back and change the day that you were born on. That is part of your concrete personal history that you cannot modify. Your other core numbers depend upon the name you were given at birth. In some circumstances, you can also calculate nicknames to give you a type of addition or amendment to your birth name. Your birth name energy stays with you for this life's journey; however, that does not mean that you cannot modify it or lessen the influence that it has over you.

In situations where the birth name causes negative feelings and associations, and there is a conscious decision made to either legally change the name or go by a different one entirely, you do actually shift the energy of your personal numerology to the direction of your new name. While you still maintain some of the energy of your previous name, you begin to take on more and more of the energy of your new name as time passes. The same applies to people who choose to change their last name due to marriage or adoption. Your original number energy will always be with you, but over time you begin to shift. When you think about the energy in a last name and how couples and families grow to share similar beliefs, values and traits, what you are noticing is the shift in energy caused by sharing the same last name.

Let's begin looking at each of the five core numbers and how to calculate your individual energy for each.

Life Path Numbers

Your life path number is hands-down the most important number in your numerology chart. While all the other numbers in numerology speak to certain aspects of your life, it is your life path number that represents the traits that you were born with and how those traits will influence your behaviors and actions as you journey through your life's purpose. You may read that there are two different numbers that share the same significance; the life path number and the birth number. Those who choose to view these two numbers as separate will note a very small change in how the numbers are calculated, which results in a difference of outcome. For the sake of simplicity in this book, I consider the life path number and the birth number to be basically the same thing, and I subscribe to the idea that there is only one true way to calculate this number using your date of birth. For this reason, you will see only a life path description, and not a "birth number" description.

For the thousands of years that we have been using numerology to discover and bring light to the innate traits and tendencies that we carry with us throughout our lives, it is the life path number that we have relied on the most heavily for insight and clarity into our true nature and true life path. The life path number is calculated using the month, date and year of your birth. From the calculation of these numbers, you can gain insight into your natural abilities, positive and negative personality traits, and the energy that drives you. To truly grow throughout this life's journey, we need to take this information, learn more about ourselves from it, and then use it to find balance, inspiration, and motivation for our individual purposes in life.

When reading the description of each number, you will find an introduction along with the life path number description. For a complete picture, it is best to take both of these components and blend them together, rather than reading and interpreting them separately.

Calculation of your life path number is simple.

For the first example, we will use the birth day December 16, 1985.

We begin by breaking down the individual numbers for the month, day and year.

1. December is the twelfth month, so it is represented by the numerals 12. We now break that down further into a one-digit number by adding the 1 and the 2 together. 12, broken down, is 1+2, which equals **3**.
2. Next, we take the date, the sixteenth, and break that down the same way. 16, broken apart, is 1+6=**7**
3. Then we do the same thing with the year, 1985. 1+9+8+5=23. Since 23 is still a double-digit number, we will now take it one step further to achieve a single-digit number.
4. 23, broken down, is 2+3=**5**.
5. Now we take each of the individual numbers and add them together. 3+7+5=15. We are looking for a single-digit number, so we will break 15 down further: 1+5=**6**.

The life path number of a person born on December 16, 1985, is **6**.

Let's try one more. This time, the date of birth is July 12, 1950.

1. First, we look at the month number of July, which is **7**.
2. Second, we look at the date, which is 12. We want to reduce this to a single digit, so we break it down into 1+2 =**3**.

3. Finally, we look at the year, 1950. 1+9+5+0=15. We take the answer, 15, and then break that down further by adding 1+5=**6**.
4. Now, we take each of the single-digit numbers for each component of the birth day and add them together. 7+3+6=16. Now, we take 16 and turn that into 1+6=**7**.

The life path number for someone born on July 12, 1950, is **7**.

The only exception to the rule about continuing to break each number down until you reach a single-digit number is when you encounter one of the "master numbers," which are 11, 22 and 33. These numbers do not get broken down further, but instead added into the total as is. These numbers also do not get broken down further when they show up as life path numbers. For example, let's calculate the life path number for the birth day November 29, 1901.

1. November is the eleventh month. Since **11** is a master number, we do not break down the components and add them together.
2. The date of birth is the twenty-ninth. 2+9=**11**. Here, since the answer is a master number, we do not need to break it down any further.
3. For the year, 1901, we add 1+9+0+1=**11**. Again, our answer is a master number and can be left as is.
4. To calculate the life path number, we take all three answers: 11+11+11=**33**. Since 33 is one of the three master numbers, we do not need to break this number down further.

The life path number of someone born on November 29, 1901, is **33**.

Destiny Numbers

The destiny number is the second of the core numbers that we will address. When we spoke of life path numbers, we talked about how that number symbolizes who and what you are, or the energy that you were born with. Now, with the destiny number, we are able to gain insight into the future. This is not a type of divination, but rather a story of the path that is laid out in front of you. It tells of the path that you must take for growth and harmony in life. The destiny number outlines your strongest and weakest traits and with that forms a path of opportunities, tasks and challenges that you will come face to face with in your lifetime.

The destiny number is derived from the name that was chosen for you at birth. The energy of your birth name tells of the road ahead of you for all your life's journey. It doesn't matter whether or not you like your birth name, or if you feel connected to it. Many people feel disconnected from the name that they were given at birth and choose to go by a different name, or even legally change it. For the purpose of calculating your destiny number, you must use the full name that was given to you at birth, even if the name you currently have is different. When calculating your destiny number:

- Do not shorten your name.
- Do not use nicknames.
- Do not add in anything extra such as junior, senior, etc.
- If your name has legally changed due to marriage or personal preferences, use your maiden name, or the name given to you at birth.
- If you were adopted as an infant, use the name that your adopted parents gave to you.

- If you were adopted as a child, use the name that was given to you at birth.
- If you are unsure of your name at birth, and have no way of finding out, use the earliest name that you remember.
- If you have a hyphenated name, consider that one name when calculating rather than two separate names.

To calculate the destiny number, we are going to use the following chart. Each letter of the alphabet is assigned a numerical value. To calculate this number, you will take each of your names individually and tally the numerical values for each letter of the name. Then, you will add the values of each of the individual names together and continue breaking it down further until you have a single-digit number, the exception of course being the master numbers 11, 22 and 33.

Let's begin with an example, and say that this person's name is John Allen Smith.

First, we will use the chart to calculate the numerical energy of each individual name.

1	2	3	4	5	6	7	8	9
A	B	C	D	E	F	G	H	I
J	K	L	M	N	O	P	Q	R
S	T	U	V	W	X	Y	Z	.

- John: J=1, O=6, H=8, N=5, so we add 1+6+8+5 and get the answer 20. 20 is a double-digit number, so let's break it down further by adding 2+0 to get the numerical value of 2. The destiny number energy associated with the name John is **2**.

- Next, we will do the middle name Allen. A=1, L=3, L=3, E=5 and N=5. We now add these numbers together. 1+3+3+5+5=17. We want to break this down further to a single digit, so we take the number 17 and turn that into 1+7=8. The destiny number energy associated with the name Allen is **8**.
- Now, we do the last name Smith. S=1, M=4, I=9, T=2, H=8. Now, we add these numbers together. 1+4+9+2+8=24. We want a single digit or master number, so we take 24 and turn that into 2+4=6. The destiny number energy associated with the name Smith is **6**.
- Finally, we take each number associated with each name and add them together. We have 2 for John, 8 for Allen and 6 for Smith. This looks like 2+8+6=16. We want a single digit or master number as the final answer, so we take 16 and break that down to 1+6=**7**.
- The destiny number for someone named John Allen Smith is **7**.

Let's do another one, this time with a longer name, Matilda Nicole Ann Smith.

- 4+1+2+9+3+4+1=24. To achieve an answer that is either a single digit or a master number, we take 24 and turn that into 2+4=6. The destiny number energy of the name Matilda is **6**.
- Since there are two middle names here that are not hyphenated, we will include them both, but add them separately. We start with Nicole. N=5, I=9, C=3, O=6, L=3, E=5. We now add up these numbers, 5+9+3+6+3+5=31. To achieve a single digit or master number answer, we take 31 and turn that into 3+1=4. The destiny number energy for the name Nicole is **4**.

- Next, we take the second middle name, Ann. A=1, N=5, N=5. We add these numbers together. 1+5+5=11. The number 11 is a master number, so there is no need to break this down further into a single-digit number. The destiny number energy of the name Ann is the master number **11**.
- Now, we do the last name Smith. S=1, M=4, I=9, T=2, H=8. Now, we add these numbers together. 1+4+9+2+8=24. We want a single digit or master number, so we take 24 and turn that into 2+4=6. The destiny number energy associated with the name Smith is **6**.
- Finally, we add the numbers associated with each name together. Matilda=6, Nicole=4, Ann=11 and Smith=6, so we have 6+4+11+6=27. We want a single digit or a master number as the final answer, so we take 27 and turn that into 2+7=9. The destiny number for the name Matilda Nicole Ann Smith is **9**.

Soul Numbers

The soul number of numerology, also called the heart's desire number, represents the thoughts, feelings and emotions that reside deep within your heart. These are the things that you yearn for, that you dream about, and that occupy your mind when you are lost in thought. These are your dreams, your aspirations, and your fears, basically all that your heart holds. The soul number helps us discover what motivates us and gives us clarity to understand the true motive behind every word and action.

Your soul number can help you get in touch with your authentic self, your energy that vibrates beneath the surface when you are able to push aside all other expectations and restrictions. This is who you are at the very core; it is the pure energy behind your thoughts and actions. Because this energy runs beneath the surface, we can consider it to be a bit of an undercurrent—not seen, but significantly impacting the surrounding waters. I like to think of this energy as fluid, like water. I also make this connection because to calculate your soul number, you are only going to use the vowels in your name. I think of vowels as the fluid letters of the alphabet. The sound they make is determined by their placement and surroundings, but without them, words cannot be formed. They move and change, but they determine the meaning and energy of the word. For example, we can look at the words read and reed. Two different spellings, and these words would have two different soul number if we were to attach a value to them. Based on the change of just one vowel, the whole energy of the word is different.

To calculate the soul number, we are going to use the same alphanumerical chart as we did with the destiny numbers, except this time we are only going to concern ourselves with the letters A, E, I, O, U and sometimes Y.*

26

1	2	3	4	5	6	7	8	9
A	B	C	D	E	F	G	H	I
J	K	L	M	N	O	P	Q	R
S	T	U	V	W	X	Y	Z	.

When calculating your soul number, you want to keep the following things in mind.

- Use your full birth name.
- Do not shorten your name, even if you most often go by a shorter form.
- Do not use nicknames, even if you most often go by one.
- If you have legally changed your name, use your original birth name.
- If you were adopted as a child, use the name you were given at birth.
- If you were adopted as an infant, use the name given to you by your adoptive parents.
- Do not add any extras such as Jr., Sr., etc.

*A special note about the letter Y. If your name contains the letter Y, include it in your calculations if, and only if, it makes a vowel sound. For example, in the name Mary, the Y makes a long E sound, so it should be included. In the name Ty, the Y makes a long I sound, so it should be included. In the name Yanni, the Y does not make a vowel sound and therefore should not be included.

To calculate the soul number, we do not need to separate each name as we did in calculating the destiny number. Instead, we will take the numerical value of each vowel in your name and add them together. From there, we will break it down further, if

27

necessary, until we have either a single digit or master number of 11, 22 or 33 as an answer. Let's begin with an example.

Tara Marie Jones:

- We first want to pull out all the vowels from the name. In **Tara Marie Jones**, you can see that there is an A, A, A, I, E, O, and E.
- Next, using the chart, we assign the correct numerical value to each vowel. A=1, I=9, E=5 and O=6. Now we add the numerical value of each vowel in the name Tara Marie Jones together. A+A+A+I+E+O+E can be translated to 1+1+1+9+5+6+5=28.
- We want either a single digit or master number as the answer, so we will take the number 28 and turn that into 2+8=10.
- Again, since the number 10 is neither a single digit nor a master number, we need to break it down further. We take the number 10 and turn that into 1+0=1.
- The soul number for Tara Marie Jones is **1**.

Let's do another, this time for Barry Yosef Smith.

- We first want to pull out all the vowels from the name. Since this name has a Y in two different places, we need to look at whether each Y is acting as a vowel or a consonant to determine if it will be included in the soul number calculation. In the name Barry, the Y has a long E sound; therefore it is acting as a vowel and should be included. In the Yosef, the Y has a consonant sound and therefore should not be included.
- So, when we highlight the vowels that we will be calculating, the name will look like this: **Barry Yosef Smith**.

- Now, let's assign numerical values to each of the vowels using the alphanumerical chart above. A=1, Y=7, O=6, E=5 and I=9.
- Now we take the vowels in the name Barry Yosef Smith and turn them into the equation A+Y+O+E+I. When we replace the numerical value for each letter, we end up with an equation that looks like 1+7+6+5+9=28.
- We want to reduce this number to either a single digit or master number, so we take the number 28 and turn it into 2+8=10.
- Again, 10 is not a single digit or a master number, so we want to break it down further into 1+0=1.
- The soul number for the name Barry Yosef Smith is **1**, which coincidentally is the same as Tara Marie Jones. These two individuals will share some things in common.

Personality Numbers

Up until this point, when calculating the different core numbers using the numerical value assigned to letters in your name, I have stipulated that you should only use your birth name for calculations. There is another theory on this, and that is that each of the group of numbers derived from your name has a major and a minor category. The major is the numerical energy of your birth name, and the minor is the numerical value of your nickname or changed name. The one time that I feel that it is really worth calculating a minor value is with the personality number. I encourage you to calculate this number using first your birth name, and then again using the name that you most commonly go by, if it is different from your birth name. I find it very interesting to look at and compare the two. With one, you have the personality traits that you were born with. I typically see these as outward traits and the way that you are generally viewed. Then, with the minor personality number, using your nickname, we can see the inner personality, the one that only the people who are the very closest to you actually get to see. This is an interesting comparison that can be quite illuminating.

The personality number tells primarily of the self we present to others. It can give you insight into how others might view you, and it can bring to light the process that you use when revealing your true self, such as in which situations you are comfortable revealing the most and becoming vulnerable and exposed. In the most basic of terms, your major personality number is your image, the energy that you put forth in public. The minor personality number is a representation of the more vulnerable side of your personality, the one you protect and might not often share with others.

To calculate your personality number, we are going to once again use the alphanumeric chart, except this time, we are concerned only with the consonants in your name. Remember that your full name should be used, and that for your major personality number you should use your birth name, and for your minor personality number, you should use the name that you most often go by. If you do not have a secondary name, then the major and primary personality numbers would be the same for you.

A special note about the letter Y. This letter can act as either a vowel or a consonant depending on its placement and the sound that it makes. For example, in the name Mary, the Y at the end has a long E sound and therefore acts as a vowel. Since we are dealing only with consonants to compute the personality number, we would not include this Y in the calculation. On the other hand, in a name like Tonya, the Y has a consonant sound, and in this case, we would include it in the calculation of the personality number.

We will begin with an example of the difference in personality numbers using the major and minor calculations for the same person. For this example, we will use Jonathan William Smith, who goes by the nickname Johnny.

1	2	3	4	5	6	7	8	9
A	B	C	D	E	F	G	H	I
J	K	L	M	N	O	P	Q	R
S	T	U	V	W	X	Y	Z	.

- First, we will work on the birth name by highlighting all the consonants in each name. We will calculate each individual name separately. **Jonathan William Smith** would have alphabetical equations that look like this:
- J+N+T+H+N (for Jonathan)
- W+L+L+M (for William)
- S+M+T+H (for Smith)
- Now, let's assign the numerical value to each equation to calculate the preliminary numbers.
- J+N+T+H+N translates into 1+5+2+8+5=21. We want either a single digit or master number as an answer, so we will take 21 and turn that into 2+1=3. The personality number for the name Jonathan is **3**.
- Next, for William, we have W+L+L+M, which translates into 5+3+3+4=15. We want either a single digit or master number as an answer, so we will break this down further into 1+5=6. The personality number for the name William is **6**.
- Finally, for the last name of Smith, we have S+M+T+H, which translates to 1+4+2+8=15. We will break this down to 1+5=6. The personality number for the name Smith is **6**.
- Now, we take each individual number and add them together. We have 3+6+6=15. We want either a single digit or a master number, so we will further break this down to 1+5=6. The personality number for Jonathan William Smith is **6**.

Now, let's do the same thing using his nickname, Johnny.

- For the name Johnny, the Y at the end takes on a long E sound. Therefore, it will be considered a vowel rather than a consonant and will not be used in calculating the minor personality number for this name.

32

- First, we pull out the consonants in the name **Johnn**y. The alphabetical equation will look like this J+H+N+N.
- Next, we assign the correct numerical value to each letter to create a new equation that looks like this: 1+8+5+5=19. We want to have either a single digit or master number as our answer, so we break this down further into 1+9=10. From there, we take 10 and turn that into 1+0=1. The personality number for the name Johnny is **1**.
- Since the middle and last names have remained unchanged from the major personality calculations, we can just plug their values in. We have Johnny which is a 1, William which is a 6 and Smith which is also a 6. The equation will look like this: 1+6+6=13.
- We want to break that 13 down further, so we add 1+3=4. The minor personality number, based on the nickname Johnny William Smith, is a **4**.

This person with this birth name and nickname has a major personality number of 6 and a minor personality number of 4.

Birth Day Number

Finally, we come to the last of the five core numbers in numerology. This number, which is the easiest to calculate, is perhaps the most influential. Each of the other core numbers looks at a very specific area of your personality and/or development. Here, with the birth day number, we gain a big-picture view of the overall energy that influences your life. It is when we take each of the other core numbers and look at them in conjunction with the birth day number that we are able to gain the greatest insight into that particular part of ourselves.

You can also use this method of calculation to give you insight into the energy and vibrations of any given day. You may find that you encounter the same challenges on every day that shares a certain number energy, for example.

To calculate your birth day number or a daily number, all you need to do is take the actual numerical date and derive the energy from that. For example, if you were born on March 1, then your birth day number is a 1. If you were born on December 8, then your birth day number is an 8. All birth day numbers should be either a single digit (1–9) or one of the master numbers of 11 or 22 (there being no circumstances in which your birth day number can be 33).

For example, if you were born on April 21, then you change that to 2+1=3. If you were born on April 22, you keep it as 22 since it is a master number.

Life Cycles: Personal Years, Essence Numbers and Pinnacle Cycles

Numerology focuses primarily on the numbers one through nine, except for the master numbers (11, 22 and 33) and karmic debt numbers (13, 14, 16 and 19). Any double-digit number that is not a master number or a karmic debt number is reduced to a single-digit number ranging from one to nine, also called the cardinal numbers. These numbers are incredibly significant, not just for their vibrational energy as they apply to your core numbers, but also in how they affect the cycles of your life. The cycles of life have a pattern to them, and it seems only natural that this pattern reflects the changing vibrations of each of the single-digit numbers. Through the use of numerology, we gain greater insight into these cycles. The three main numerology cycles that we will look at are the nine-year cycle of change, essence numbers, and the pinnacle cycles.

Personal Years and the Nine-Year Cycle of Change

As you learn more about numerology, you will begin to notice a pattern of growth. The very nature of numbers tells us that growth is essential. A child on their ninth birthday is a completely different person than they were on their first. We can say the same concerning the years of our life cycles. When you open yourself up to the opportunities for growth and development, you will find that you are not the same person in year nine that you were in year one—and this is a good thing. The nine-year cycles allow us time, room and opportunity to grow and develop on a spiritual level.

Each year of the nine-year cycle has its own energy. Every beginning means that there was an end to something. One door closes before another opens, and as you make your way through each of the years, you will find that some years are easy, while others prove to be more challenging and difficult. This cycle is a perfect reminder that "to everything there is a season." During this cycle, you might feel that the energy intensifies as you approach year nine. The closer you come to the end of the cycle, the more you will be pushed to do what is necessary to fulfill your soul's purpose. Nearing completion of a current cycle also reminds us that where we stand now, and the next phase of life, is a direct result of our choices in the past. Here, you have the chance to face the past, make peace and find closure in a way that helps you shape the future that you see for yourself. During each year of this cycle you have the opportunity to decide what comes next, but you can only do so by acknowledging the influence that your past has had upon this very moment and all future moments. Where you are right now is a direct result of everything you have ever thought, felt, achieved, accomplished, feared or lost.

In life cycle patterns, we see that the first year brings about birth and newness, while the ninth year brings about the same energy of completion. During the ninth year, we have completed one cycle, and as we begin to say goodbye to the thoughts, actions and behaviors that have defined the previous nine years, we find that in essence we are preparing ourselves for the next cycle. Becoming consciously aware of these cycles in life will help to prepare you for the change in energy that comes with each year and each new cycle. It will also help you to transition from one to another without feeling as though something has been left incomplete or unresolved from the previous cycle.

Realizing this is important, because you have to release yourself from the previous life cycle—even if it was the best of your life so far—so that you can move forward. This means releasing yourself on all levels, including physically, emotionally, mentally and spiritually. If you refuse to acknowledge and accept the necessity of this release, you will likely find yourself reliving the same mistakes repeatedly. You will be stuck in old patterns while feeling as though there is no escape. However, the truth is that you, and you alone, create your reality. The vibrational energy of each year of the cycle helps guide you in deciding what to embrace and what to avoid, along with recognizing what is most important and where to focus your energy.

Where you are in the nine-year cycle is often referred to as your "personal" year. Calculating your personal year is very simple, and involves combining the numbers from the month and date of your birth with the numerical energy of the current calendar year.

For example, let's calculate the personal year energy in 2017 for someone born on August 16.

- We make note that August is the eighth month. Next, we want to calculate the numbers in an equation that looks like this: $8+16+2017=2041$.
- Next, we break down the answer in an equation that looks like this: $2+0+4+1=7$.
- A person born on August 16 has a personal year number of 7 during the year of 2017.

For a more in-depth understanding of the meaning of your personal year number, you can read through the descriptions of each number a little later in this book. There are some differences in how to apply the numbers to your personal year, but you will be able to assess the general energy associated with each. To get you started, I'm providing a simplified description of how each numerical energy will manifest during each personal year here:

Personal Year 1

Having a one as a personal year number signifies an incredibly exciting time in your life. The one year is a clean slate, a time to start anew, especially if you have done the work to properly release the energy of the previous cycle before entering this one. You will be presented with new opportunities. This is the time to set goals and take action. We can think of the one year as being youthful, and with youth comes energy and optimism. Now is the time to set into action your plans for the future. The potential downfall of the personal year one is that your ego and naïveté can get in the way. If you let this happen, you might miss out on opportunities that will not present themselves again until the beginning of the next nine-year cycle. Stay focused and grounded while branching out and reaching for all the possibility that this year holds.

Personal Year 2

After year one, year two gives you the opportunity to relax a little and focus on yourself more than outside influences. This year holds an energy of companionship, compassion and kindness. While last year was a flurry of energy, this year allows you to enjoy warmth and familiarity. Now is the time to work on making relationships stronger, or forming new ones. The two year is also a good time to enter into new partnerships, whether they be business or personal.

Personal Year 3

Those relationships you strengthened and the new friendships you formed in year two will become especially important in year three. While this year isn't all play and no work, it is a year of celebration and community. You might find yourself becoming more social this year, or opening in other ways, such as through creative outlets. In year two, you relaxed and recovered from the energy in year one. Now, that energy is back, but it is a little more mature and centered. This is the year to loosen your control a little bit and let the energy of fate and destiny take the reins every now and then. This doesn't mean to throw all caution to the wind; however, beautiful things can happen when you let go of a little bit of control.

Personal Year 4
During year four, things start to get a little more serious. This is a year about grounding yourself, making commitments and following through. This is the year of building your foundations. If we think of the nine-year cycle as being representative of the life cycle, we can view the four year as being a young adult who has just settled into a career or is starting a family. Now is not the time for whimsy or laziness. Instead, the focus is on clarity, hard work, goals and organization. You might find at times that you really need to push yourself forward in year four. The energy can seem mundane and challenging at the same time, but this is not the year to slack off. What you put into this year will pay off. Keep this in mind during those times when you are lacking the energy or initiative to put in the necessary work.

Personal Year 5
Year five is still serious business; however the energy is greatly different than it was in year four. In year five, you begin to see the potential for growth from all your hard work in year four. New opportunities will present themselves, and it is especially important to let go of old thought patterns that might be holding you back. This is the year of personal freedom and trusting your intuition. The chains of the past year are being released and there is incredible opportunity to take your life in the direction that you want it to go. At times, it may seem like things are flying at you with lightning speed, which can be overwhelming and

stressful. Remember to stay grounded and true to yourself and you will be able to navigate this exciting year with ease.

Personal Year 6
Year six is all about self-care and nurturing. You have passed the midway point in the nine-year cycle, and along the way there are sure to have been changes and challenges that have tested your spirit and left you tired. This is the year to pull it all in and focus on what is closest to you. This includes taking time to nurture yourself, your family and those closest to you. Themes for this year include taking care of your health, both mental and physical, giving yourself permission to do things that you enjoy, centering, grounding, warmth and security.

Personal Year 7
This is the year of introspection. It is time to quiet the noise from the outside and focus on what is inside of you. This year personal growth and spiritual development are at the forefront. This period of quiet and reflection is important for growth and self-awareness. You might find that at times the energy of this year feels a little dark and isolated. Trust that this is a good thing. You need this time to strengthen your sense of purpose. Do not worry that periods of loneliness will last too long. When you are ready and open, others will be drawn to your steady calmness and self-assurance.

Personal Year 8
The last couple of years have been the downtime that was necessary for you to do the work on the soul level. You are nearing the end of the nine-year cycle, which means that it is time to reap the rewards and begin preparing for the transition from one cycle to the next. Consider this year your harvest. All the hard work that you have put in is paying off this year. There is a strong increase in energy this year, and you will likely find yourself very busy, if not physically then at least mentally. There

are lots of decisions to be made, and you will find yourself the center of attention. The energy that you put into this year will strongly affect the path that this cycle of life will take to reach its completion.

Personal Year 9

The theme of this year is out with the old so that you have room for the new. This is a year of discarding what no longer serves a purpose in your life, and of taking stock of what is important and protecting it. This is also a time to look seriously at what changes need to be made. If you do not do this readily, there is a good chance that the universe will force you into it. Because this is a year of shedding and release, it is not necessarily a good time to start something new. If you are looking at a new business venture, considering a long-term relationship, or looking to start a family, it is better to hold off for a year until the energy is more suited to beginnings than endings. Remember this year that endings are a necessary prelude to beginnings. Doors do not close without others opening, and clearing out the negative only makes room for you to welcome the positive.

Essence Numbers

The next cycle-based numbers I would like to discuss are called essence numbers. Essence numbers are a bit more complex then personal year numbers. Essence numbers are calculated based on the letters in your birth name, with the energy of each numerical value influencing your life for a corresponding number of years. Essence numbers are not the numbers that you read to get a broad overview of your life. Instead, essence numbers provide us with subtleties that will influence your life for a certain number of years. The energy of the essence number should be used in combination with other cycle numbers, such as your personal year number, to help give you insight and clarity into the factors influencing your life. Essence numbers can also be used as a forecast into the future. For example, if you know that the energy of the number four is going to be with you for the next year, you can begin to mentally prepare for the hard work and challenges that are associated with that number.

Essence numbers are one of the more difficult numbers to calculate, at least in my opinion. I am going to go through a detailed description of how to do so, but would also like to suggest that when you are calculating your own, or someone else's, you do a quick search for a printable worksheet that will simplify the process.

To calculate your essence numbers, you will use the letters in your full name, creating three distinct categories: first name, middle name and last name. For the sake of calculating essence numbers, your name needs to fit neatly into these three categories. That means that if you have a double first name, such as Mary Ann, you should include the letters for both first names together in the first name category. The same applies if you have more than one middle or last name. Hyphenated names also count as one name together. For example, if your

42

name was Mary Ann Elizabeth Jane Smith-Miller, you would categorize your names as Mary Ann being the first (if they are both used as a first name and not a first and middle name combination), Elizabeth Jane together as the middle name, and Smith-Miller together as the last.

Once you have your name split into the three categories, you can begin assigning numbers. When calculating essence numbers, the numerical values not only represent a certain energy, but also indicate how long that energy is going to be with you. In the case of the name Mary, the letter M has the numerical value of four, and therefore the energy of the letter M will be with you for four years before you move onto the second letter in the name Mary, which is an A. The letter A has a numerical value of one, meaning the energy will stay with you for one year before moving on to the letter R, and so forth.

You are going to calculate each of your three names in this manner, and then calculate the three values for a given year to come up with your essence number. For an example, let's use the name Steven Harris Miller. We will need the following alphanumeric chart to help us.

1	2	3	4	5	6	7	8	9
A	B	C	D	E	F	G	H	I
J	K	L	M	N	O	P	Q	R
S	T	U	V	W	X	Y	Z	.

It is important to note that when calculating your essence number, you need to start at birth and continue calculating until you reach your current age. We will use a simplified chart to help organize the information.

Key: A=age, FN=first name, MN=middle name, LN=last name, FV=value associated with first name, MV=value associated with middle name, LV=value associated with last name.

We will start with the first name Steven. I like to begin by jotting down the numerical value associated with each letter.

S=1, T=2, E=5, V=4, E=5, N=5.

The number associated with each letter indicates how long the energy of that letter/number is going to influence Steven's life. Each letter stays in place for the number of years that matches its numerical value. For example, S has a value of one and will influence Steven's life for one year. Then the influence will shift to the T, which has a numerical value of two and will influence Steven's life for two years. From there, we move on to the E, which has a value of five and will influence Steven's life for five years before the energy of the letter V enters and so on. Once the energy of the last letter of the name passes, in this case the N/5, the cycle begins over again with the first letter of the name.

Using the key above, let's begin making our chart.

A	FN	FV

0–1   S   1
(The letter S has a numerical value of one, so for the next year, we will move on to the next letter in the name, which is T.)
1–2   T   2
(The letter T has a numerical value of two, so we will use this letter and its energy for two consecutive years in the chart before moving on to the third letter in the name, which is E.)
2–3   T   2
3–4   E   5

(The letter E has a numerical energy of 5, so we will use this for 5 years.)

4–5	E	5
5–6	E	5
6–7	E	5
7–8	E	5
8–9	V	4

(Now, we transition to V for 4 consecutive years.)

9–10	V	4
10–11	V	4
11–12	V	4
12–13	E	5

(The next letter is E, so we will have that energy for 5 years.)

13–14	E	5
14–15	E	5
15–16	E	5
16–17	E	5
17–18	N	5

(Finally, we have the letter N, which will last another 5 years.)

18–19	N	5
19–20	N	5
20–21	N	5
21–22	N	5

By completing this chart, we see that the numerical energy of the name Steven has a cycle that takes 22 years to complete before it starts over again.

Now, let's take the work that we just did and add in the values for the middle name.

A	FN	MN	FV	MV
0–1	S	H	1	8
1–2	T	H	2	8

45

2–3	T	H	2	8
3–4	E	H	5	8

(We see here that even though the numbers for the first name are changing, the H from the middle name is still present because it must be included for 8 consecutive years.)

4–5	E	H	5	8
5–6	E	H	5	8
6–7	E	H	5	8
7–8	E	H	5	8
8–9	V	A	4	1

(Here we see a transition of numbers.)

9–10	V	R	4	9
10–11	V	R	4	9
11–12	V	R	4	9
12–13	E	R	5	9
13–14	E	R	5	9
14–15	E	R	5	9
15–16	E	R	5	9
16–17	E	R	5	9
17–18	N	R	5	9
18–19	N	R	5	9

(The middle name has two consecutive Rs; the second starts here.)

19–20	N	R	5	9
20–21	N	R	5	9
21–22	N	R	5	9
22–23	S	R	1	9

(The first name cycle is complete, so it starts over.)

23–24	T	R	2	9
24–25	T	R	2	9
25–26	E	R	5	9
26–27	E	R	5	9
27–28	E	I	5	9

(We move on to the next letter of the middle name.)

28–29	E	I	5	9

A			
29–30 E	I	5	9
30–31 V	I	4	9
31–32 V	I	4	9
32–33 V	I	4	9
33–34 V	I	4	9
34–35 E	I	5	9
35–36 E	I	5	9
36–37 E	S	5	1

(The final letter of the middle name.)

So, you can see that while the first name Steven has a cycle of twenty-two years, the middle name Harris is significantly longer at thirty-seven years. We almost go through two complete first name cycles before finishing one middle name cycle.

Now, let's complete our chart with the last name Miller.

A	FN	MN	LN	FV	MV	LV
0–1	S	H	M	1	8	4
1–2	T	H	M	2	8	4
2–3	T	H	M	2	8	4
3–4	E	H	M	5	8	4
4–5	E	H	I	5	8	9
5–6	E	H	I	5	8	9
6–7	E	H	I	5	8	9
7–8	E	H	I	5	8	9
8–9	V	A	I	4	1	9
9–10	V	R	I	4	9	9
10–11	V	R	I	4	9	9
11–12	V	R	I	4	9	9
12–13	E	R	I	5	9	9
13–14	E	R	L	5	9	3
14–15	E	R	L	5	9	3
15–16	E	R	L	5	9	3

16–17 E	R	L	5	9	3

(The second L of the last name begins here.)

17–18 N	R	L	5	9	3
18–19 N	R	L	5	9	3
19–20 N	R	E	5	9	5
20–21 N	R	E	5	9	5
21–22 N	R	E	5	9	5
22–23 S	R	E	1	9	5
23–24 T	R	E	2	9	5
24–25 T	R	R	2	9	9
25–26 E	R	R	5	9	9
26–27 E	R	R	5	9	9
27–28 E	I	R	5	9	9
28–29 E	I	R	5	9	9
29–30 E	I	R	5	9	9
30–31 V	I	R	4	9	9
31–32 V	I	R	4	9	9
32–33 V	I	R	4	9	9
33–34 V	I		4	9	
34–35 E	I		5	9	
35–36 E	I		5	9	
36–37 E	S		5	1	

From this chart, we see that the last name of Miller has a thirty-three-year cycle before it starts over.

You would continue each cycle of your name until you reached your current age to determine your current essence number.

In our example, let's say that Steven Harris Smith is twenty-five years old and wants to know what his essence number is. We would find the age line that reads 25–26 and calculate all the values. Here is the example from our chart above:

A	FN	MN	LN	FV	MV	LV

25–26 E   R   R   5   9   9

In this case, we will add the values of 5+9+9=23

We want to reduce this to a single digit, so we then take 23 and turn it into 2+3=5.

Steven Harris Miller's essence number at the age of 25 is 5.

If the sum of your essence year numbers equals one of the karmic debt numbers of 13, 14, 16 or 19, you should apply that energy to the year in addition to the resulting single-digit number.

To find out what your essence number means, and how it will influence your life this year, simply read over the number descriptions and refer back to the personal year number descriptions. Each number's energy does not change drastically; the significance is more in how you are applying it in each situation.

Pinnacle Cycles

Pinnacle cycles are the longest cycles that you will encounter in basic numerology. During the course of an average lifespan, there are four distinct cycles that appear. These cycles represent the major lessons, and the circumstances surrounding them, that will be prominent during each of the four phases of life.

The first pinnacle cycle starts at birth and reaches completion somewhere in your late twenties to early thirties. In other words, the first pinnacle cycle takes you through childhood and lands you at the beginning of true adulthood. Yes, you are technically an adult in your late teens and early twenties, but this is still a period of great growth and development. The type of adulthood you experience after that phase is typically very different, and the pinnacle cycles represent that.

The second and third pinnacle cycles each last nine years. These cycles occur during major transitional periods in your adult life. The second pinnacle cycle generally consists of your thirties, while the third takes place in your forties. Each decade of life comes with its unique challenges and lessons, and the pinnacle cycles help to illuminate that and guide us through. Finally, the fourth pinnacle cycle begins in your late forties or early fifties and continues for the rest of your life.

To understand which pinnacle cycle you are in, and then calculate your personal numerical energy for that cycle, the first step is to determine what your life path number is. If you haven't already calculated your life path number when reading the previous chapter, you can find it by simply adding the numbers in your complete birth day. For example, if your birth day is January 2, 1980 (1/2/1980), you would find your life path number using the following equation: 1+2+1980.

The first two numbers of that equation are easy, but we want to simply the year 1980 by turning it into 1+9+8+0=18. To further simplify it, we take 18 and turn that into 1+8=9. We can now substitute the number 9 in for 1980 in the equation:

1+2+9=12

Since the number 12 is neither a single digit nor a master number, we will reduce it one step further by adding 1+2=3.

If you were born on January 2, 1980, your life path number is 3.

Now, you can use your life path number to determine exactly when you transition from one pinnacle cycle to the next, using the following chart:

Life Path Number	First Pinnacle Cycle	Second Pinnacle Cycle	Third Pinnacle Cycle	Fourth Pinnacle Cycle
1	Birth to Age 35	Age 35–44	Age 44–53	Age 53+
2	Birth to Age 34	Age 34–43	Age 43–52	Age 52+
3	Birth to Age 33	Age 33–42	Age 42–51	Age 51+
4	Birth to Age 32	Age 32–41	Age 41–50	Age 50+
5	Birth to Age 31	Age 31–40	Age 40–49	Age 49+
6	Birth to Age 30	Age 30–39	Age 39–48	Age 48+
7	Birth to Age 29	Age 29–38	Age 38–47	Age 47+
8	Birth to Age 28	Age 28–37	Age 37–46	Age 46+
9	Birth to Age 27	Age 27–36	Age 36–45	Age 45+
11	Birth to Age 34	Age 34–43	Age 43–52	Age 52+
22	Birth to Age 32	Age 32–41	Age 41–50	Age 50+

Once you know when your pinnacle cycles begin and end, and which pinnacle cycle you are currently in, or will be transitioning into, you can calculate the numerical energy associated with your individual pinnacle cycle. With each pinnacle, there is a distinct way of calculating the associated number.

We will use our above example of someone born on January 2, 1980, to illustrate how to calculate each cycle. We know that this person has a life path number of three, so we can see that for this person, the first pinnacle cycle begins at birth and lasts until the age of 33. The second pinnacle cycle is from ages 33–42, the third pinnacle cycle is from the ages of 42–51, and the fourth pinnacle cycle begins at the age of 51 and continues for the rest of their life.

To calculate the energy associated with the first pinnacle cycle, you only need to add the month and the day of your birth date. In the example of January 2, 1980, we would add 1+2=3. The first pinnacle energy for this person is 3.

To calculate the second pinnacle cycle energy, you will add the day and the year of your birth day. In this example, we add 2+1980.

We want to break down the large number of 1980, so we add it in together in the equation 1+9+8+0=18. We want this reduced further, so we turn 18 into 1+8=9. We can now take that 9 and substitute it for 1980 in the equation.

2+9=11. Since 11 is a master number, we do not need to reduce it further. The second pinnacle cycle energy for this person is 11.

To calculate the third pinnacle cycle energy, we add the numbers associated with pinnacle cycle one and pinnacle cycle two. In this example, that would be 3+11=14.

The number 14 is a karmic debt number, and although we will reduce it further to 1+4=5, leaving 5 as the numerical energy associated with this person's third pinnacle cycle, we should take note that this person will likely be dealing with some of the karmic debt issues associated with the number 14 during this time as well.

Finally, to calculate the numerical energy of the fourth pinnacle cycle, we add the month and the year of the birth date. We know from the above example that the year 1980 reduces to the number 9, so we can go ahead and substitute that in for 1980 in the equation 1+9=10. We will now break this down further by taking 10 and turning it into 1+0=1. This person's fourth pinnacle number is 1.

To determine how your numbers will affect you in your pinnacle cycles, you will want to read the descriptions of each number in this book. However, when it comes to pinnacle cycles, the energy of the number will alter slightly depending upon the pinnacle cycle that you are in. For instance, if you have the number 1 for both your first and your second pinnacle cycles, the base energy will be the same, but there will be differences in how that energy affects you. With that in mind, I would like to supply a quick keyword reference for how each numerical energy acts in each of the pinnacle cycles.

The Number One
- First Pinnacle Cycle: Independence, Self-Reliance, Determination, Resilience, Inner Strength
- Second Pinnacle Cycle: Energy, Speed, Personal Growth, Hard Work, Clarity, Effort, Personal Responsibility
- Third Pinnacle Cycle: Goals, Leadership, Adversity, Strength, Challenge
- Fourth Pinnacle Cycle: Dreams, Goals, Accomplishments, Gratification

The Number Two

- First Pinnacle Cycle: Peace, Support, Diplomacy, Intuition, Patience, Calm, Self-Assurance, Advisor, Counsel
- Second Pinnacle Cycle: Peace, Balance, Harmony, Compromise, Mediation
- Third Pinnacle Cycle: Shyness, Self-Consciousness, Timidity, Reaching Out, Inner Voice, Trusting Yourself
- Fourth Pinnacle Cycle: Appreciation, Beauty, Arts, Insight, Fluidity

The Number Three

- First Pinnacle Cycle: Creativity, Fluidity, Awareness, Expanded Perspective, Arts
- Second Pinnacle Cycle: Energy, Social, Happiness, Friendships, Luck, Fortune
- Third Pinnacle Cycle: Hard Work, Discipline, Structure, Rigidity, Challenge
- Fourth Pinnacle Cycle: Creativity, Energy Flow, Arts, Creative Outlets, Pursuing Passions

The Number Four

- First Pinnacle Cycle: Diligence, Dependability, Hard Work, Determination, Organization
- Second Pinnacle Cycle: Responsibility, Perseverance, Burden of Others, Pillar of Strength, Foundation
- Third Pinnacle Cycle: Hard Work Paying Off, Strong Foundations, Diligence, Limits, Attention to Detail
- Fourth Pinnacle Cycle: Nurturing, Fruits of Labor, Releasing Control, Appreciating the Process

The Number Five

- First Pinnacle Cycle: Experience, Adventure, Expression, Expansion, Social, Society, Travel, Articulation
- Second Pinnacle Cycle: Grounding, Settling Down, Staying the Course, Flightiness, Undecided
- Third Pinnacle Cycle: Acceptance, Unconditional Love, Empathy, Spirituality, Giving, Self-Acceptance
- Fourth Pinnacle Cycle: Developing Natural Talents, Setting Guidelines and Limits, Self-Discovery in a Controlled Setting,

The Number Six

- First Pinnacle Cycle: Closeness, Family, Relationships, Nurture, Love, Bonding, Sacrifice, Caregiving
- Second Pinnacle Cycle: Life Foundations Formed, Commitment, Personal Conflict, Resolution, Compromise, Adjustment
- Third Pinnacle Cycle: Compassion, Healing, Unifying, Leadership, Examples, Business, Role Models
- Fourth Pinnacle Cycle: Feeling Pulled in Too Many Directions, Meddling, Intrusive, Respecting Boundaries, Understanding Your Place in the World

The Number Seven

- First Pinnacle Cycle: Introspection, Existential Thought, Intuition, Self-Knowledge, Questions, Spirituality
- Second Pinnacle Cycle: Decisions, Path Choosing, Specialization, Intuition, Knowledge, Accountability
- Third Pinnacle Cycle: Opportunity for Spiritual Growth, Judgment, Prejudice, Isolation, Sarcasm as a Defense, Opening One's Self
- Fourth Pinnacle Cycle: Perfection Versus Reality, Loosening Expectations, Loving Yourself

The Number Eight
- First Pinnacle Cycle: Success, Judgment, Opportunity, Foresight, Knowledge, Business, Completion, Harvest
- Second Pinnacle Cycle: Goals, Clarity, Stability, Accomplishments, Confidence, Overcome
- Third Pinnacle Cycle: Harmony, Balance, Duality of Spiritual and Physical Self, Consciousness, Life's Work
- Fourth Pinnacle Cycle: Reflective Thought, Balance Between Earth and Spirit, Balance, Staying Away from Extremes

The Number Nine
- First Pinnacle Cycle: Energy, Sharing, Activist, Strong Voice, Opinionated, Support, Career
- Second Pinnacle Cycle: Business Success, Financial Growth, Artistic Pursuits, Accomplishment, Challenge Overcome with Determination
- Third Pinnacle Cycle: Compassion, Empathy, Giving, Charity, Acceptance, Guidance
- Fourth Pinnacle Cycle: Knowledge, Truth, Success, Acknowledgement, Sharing

The Number Eleven
- First Pinnacle Cycle: Spirituality, Consciousness, Intuition, Higher Self, Connection, Searching, Burden, Abundance
- Second Pinnacle Cycle: Experience, Surrender, Release, Following the Flow of Energy, Open Mindedness
- Third Pinnacle Cycle: Not Being Grounded on the Physical Plane, Too Involved in Spiritual Matters, Grounding, Centering, Unbalance, Clumsiness
- Fourth Pinnacle Cycle: Intuition, Creativity, Innovation, New Ideas, Invention, Rewards

- First Pinnacle Cycle: Power, Struggle, Manifestation, Focused Energy, Confusion, Grounding
- Second Pinnacle Cycle: Dreams, Goals, Manifestation, Thinking Big, Determination, Materialization
- Third Pinnacle Cycle: Support, Struggle, Work, Potential, Extremes
- Fourth Pinnacle Cycle: Thinking Big, Long Term Goals, Big Picture, Staying on Path

Pythagorean Arrows: Lines of Individuality and Circles of Frustration

After making it this far into the book, you know by now that the art and science of numerology isn't just about adding a few numbers and then having all the answers. Just like your personality and spirit are multifaceted aspects of your self, so are the different numerical energies that are attached to you through your birth date and your name. Much of what we have covered so far has been how single numbers affect your life on different levels. When reading your numerology chart, you want to take all the numbers into consideration. We can think of your numerology numbers as a word. Each letter has a sound on its own and affects the word in a significant way; however, to read the complete word, we need to know how to blend those letters together to make it all work.

Here, with the Pythagorean Arrows, we start to go a little deeper into the "blending" of numerology. Rather than just one number, you are going to discover a sequence of numbers that are either present, in the form of lines of individuality, or absent, in the form of circles of frustration. The Pythagorean Arrows give you greater insight into your personality, including your strong traits and your weak traits.

I like to play around with the Pythagorean Arrows more than other parts of numerology because I feel that there is a little more space to do so. For instance, there is only one way to calculate your life path number, but there are multiple ways of using the Pythagorean Arrows to gain insight into your life and journey in this incarnation.

For the sake of our example here, we are going to use the birth date as our guiding numbers, mostly because it is the simplest and most commonly used. When and if you want to, you can take this method and try it using the numbers in your birth name or nickname. I like to do comparative charts on people who have changed their names to give a "then and now" snapshot. Use your intuition to guide how you use these arrows and you will be given the information that you need.

3	6	9
2	5	8
1	4	7

To use the Pythagorean Arrows, we need a simple number grid organized like this:

Now what we need is a birth date to work with. Let's choose November 29, 1955.

First, we want to separate out each number in this birth date so that it stands alone. Our sequence in this example will look like this: 1, 1, 2, 9, 1, 9, 5, 5.

Next, you will take the three-by-three grid that you created and write each of these numbers in the appropriate spot. If a number occurs more than once, write it in the appropriate box as many times as it occurs in the given sequence.

When adding the numbers from the example sequence, we will have a grid that looks like this. Notice that if a number assigned to a box does not appear in the sequence, the box was left entirely empty.

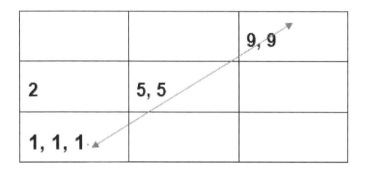

Notice that the numbers 1, 5 and 9 appeared multiple times and that we can draw an arrow through them. This indicates a set of numbers that have energies that combine to have a certain influence on your life. While the number 2 is present and should be noted, we are not able to draw a straight line connecting it with two other numbers. For the purpose of arrows of individuality and circles of frustrations, we need three consecutive cells, either horizontal, vertical or diagonal.

Here, let's try it again with a different date, February 10, 1973.

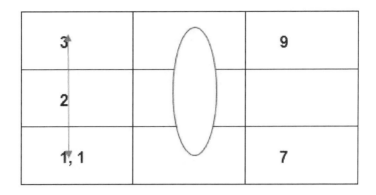

We first break the birth date down into the number sequence 2, 1, 0, 1, 9, 7, 3. Zero is not included in this chart, so we can disregard it. Then, we place each number into the appropriate square.

We can see that there is an arrow in the row that contains the numbers 1, 2 and 3. We can also see that no numbers were present in the row that would contain 4, 5 and 6. This means that there is an absence of these energies in this person's chart, otherwise known as a circle of frustration.

The next question you will have after you draw your grid and fill it in is, what do these combinations mean? Here are the guidelines on how to interpret the arrows of individuality and circles of frustration.

Each arrow or circle has a certain energy associated with it, except for a circle in the vertical row of 1–2–3. This combination as a circle of frustration is not applied at the current time. You take the energy of each combination and apply it as a strong point if it is present. If it is not, you look at how the absence of these qualities affects you, or the person that you are reading for.

Combination Meaning

1–2–3

This combination indicates qualities of a good planner, someone who likes organization and lists. This person can see the benefits of laying out a plan and strategizing. Expect this person to thrive on routine and be successful in business ventures.

4–5–6

This combination indicates a strong sense of determination, willpower and drive. The person with this combination in their chart is one who will set their sights on something and not rest until they have achieved success.

7–8–9

This is someone who has a positive outlook on life. They have the ability to see past the immediate future and focus their energy on long term goals and successes.

1–4–7

This combination will be present in someone who places high value upon their physical health and fitness. You can expect this person to enjoy physical activity and be competitive.

2–5–8

This set of numbers indicates someone who is emotionally sensitive and in touch with their higher self. People with this arrow often seek out creative endeavors and may even make a career out of them.

3–6–9

This is a person who is likely to be considered an intellectual. They like to think critically and deeply. They believe that knowledge is power, and the more the better.

1–5–9

This diagonal set of numbers indicates someone who has steadfast patience. This is the person who can wait it through and who knows that patience and perseverance pay off.

3–5–7

This combination is considered to be the highest in terms of spiritual energy and connection. A person with this energy is likely to be drawn to religious and spiritual matters and hold that part of their life in high regard. They seek out a more complete understanding of the duality between physical incarnation and spiritual self.

Connecting the Past, Present and Future: Karmic Debt and Karmic Lessons

While the core numbers of numerology give us the most insight and understanding into ourselves, they do not act alone. In fact, if you were to go for a professional numerology reading, there are many numbers that would come into play. While the core numbers are significant enough to stand on their own, there are other numbers that are just below the surface, dancing and interacting with each other, which results in an influence on your core numbers. When you are learning numerology, it is best to begin by understanding the core numbers and how they affect the individual on their own. However, once you begin to understand that, it is time to start looking at some of the subtler number energies that also have an impact on our lives.

Two of these subtler energies involve karma, or your soul's "residue" from past incarnations. With each incarnation, we grow and experience new things. We have to realize that while our soul and spirit is the same, how we choose to act and who we choose to be in our earthly bodies will very likely be different through each incarnation. After all, what would be the point of returning to this life to be the same person and experience the same life over and over again? This means that at some point in a past incarnation, you have likely done things that were not righted by the time your spirit left your body. Your soul holds onto these things as karma, and you will continue to face them throughout each incarnation until they are amended.

In numerology, karma shows up on your chart in two ways. The first is in the form of karmic debt. Not everyone has these numbers on their chart, but when you do, you will notice that they have a significant influence in your life. This is your chance to make amends for wrongdoings from the past and to grow spiritually from the experience. Secondly, we have karmic lessons. These are not quite as obvious when looking at a numerology chart, but most everyone has at least one. In this section, we will discuss the difference between these two sets of numbers, and how to easily calculate their values and understand their meanings.

Karmic Debt

Of these numbers, I feel that the karmic debt number can be the most significant. In numerology, it is believed that we are all beings on a spiritual plane, and that we incarnate into a physical body for spiritual growth, experience and to learn lessons. The day that your soul chooses to incarnate and the name that you are given at birth have a major effect on the course this incarnation will take. It is also believed that we incarnate multiple times, through numerous lives. Sometimes, during an incarnation, we make mistakes and either maliciously or unintentionally cause harm to others. Other times there were lessons that were meant to be learned that were not completed. At the end of the incarnation, these things do not simply go away; rather, they adhere to your soul so that you will have the chance to grow from these experiences in a future life.

There are certain numbers in numerology that indicate a karmic debt, or in other words, a lesson to be learned or a situation to be rectified. Your soul has held onto something from the past that needs to come to completion. Karmic debt numbers differ from the core numbers in that not everyone has them. There is no one way to calculate your karmic debt. You know that you have one when one of these numbers shows up somewhere in your life, or in your calculations of the core numbers. Karmic debt numbers are mostly related to birth day numbers and personality numbers, but they can show up anywhere.

The karmic debt numbers are 13, 14, 16 and 19. There are two ways that a karmic number can show up in a numerology reading. The first is if you have one of these numbers as your birth day. For example, if you were born on June 13, the thirteen as your birth day number indicates that you have the karmic debt associated with that number and that those issues will need to be dealt with in this lifetime.

The second way that one of these numbers can show up in any section of your reading is if they occur as a sum before further breaking the number down into a single digit. For example, suppose you were to calculate the destiny number of the name Ned. According to the alphanumeric chart, N=5, E=5 and D=4, and thus 5+5+4=14. Since you are calculating the destiny number and 14 is not a master number, you would take that number and further reduce it to a single digit by adding the 1+4 to get a destiny number of 5. The number 14 is not your destiny number, but it does appear as a sum before further reducing the number down to a single digit. This means that the energy of the karmic debt number is strong within the destiny category, and the karmic energy of this number should be applied to the overall reading as well. If you have one of the following numbers in your life as a result of further reducing a double-digit number, you need to pay attention to the karmic debt energy of that number throughout your life.

- The number 4 as a result of reducing 13 in the form of 1+3=4.
- The number 5 as a result of reducing 14 in the form of 1+4=5.
- The number 7 as a result of reducing 16 in the form of 1+6=7.

- The number 1 as a result of reducing 19 in the form of 1+9=10, and then 1+0=1.

Each of the karmic debt numbers has an energy of its own. Here is a description of each.

Thirteen

If this shows up for you, you might be thinking about how the number thirteen is considered unlucky and a curse, so of course there is negative karmic energy associated with it. I ask you to brush that aside, because first of all, lessons are never curses, but rather opportunities for growth, and second, this number is here because of your past behaviors and the good news is that it isn't that difficult to recognize the areas in your life where you can make amends.

When the karmic debt number thirteen is present, it represents a previous lifetime in which you may not have given your best effort. The typical keywords that are associated with the number thirteen are lazy, stubborn, always seeing self as the victim, negativity, rigidness, blame and control. Keep in mind that these aren't necessarily traits that you currently have, but rather ones that you had in a previous incarnation, which you must now make amends for. You may have been seen as someone who avoided doing their share of the work, but still took credit for it. You may have been someone whose laziness and lack of drive impacted the lives of others in a negative way. People with the number thirteen in their charts often had previous incarnations where they were controlling and quick to place blame as a way to cover their own lack of effort. A typical archetype might be the demanding, controlling boss who overworks his employees, yet underpays them and takes the credit for himself. Meanwhile, when things go wrong, he is quick to shove the responsibility onto someone else. (This is just an example to help you understand the type of karmic debt that the number thirteen embodies.)

To make amends for this karmic debt that you carry, begin by evaluating your life and determining if there is any area where you should be taking more responsibility. Make a conscious effort to follow things through and not take shortcuts, and realize that your own shortcomings are yours to claim and not the fault of anyone else. Use your energy in this life to lift people up and support them, rather than using them as stepping stones to your own success. Become acutely aware of the impact of both your thoughts and actions upon others. The number thirteen is about the need to own up and accept personal responsibility in this life.

Fourteen

If you have the number fourteen show up in your chart, it serves as an indicator that you have a karmic debt to repay for certain actions in your past. This number suggests that in a past incarnation, you were selfish in ways that hurt other people. This selfishness often manifested itself as excessiveness in at least one area of your life. The number fourteen is a strong indicator that there could have been some type of addiction that took precedence over the people in your life. This dependence could have been on anything from drugs or alcohol to sex and money.

People with a karmic debt number fourteen might also have been stuck on a sense of personal freedom, always needing to be free to do whatever they wanted, with whoever they wanted, whenever they wanted to do it. You can easily see that this would be destructive behavior for any long-term relationship, be it with a romantic partner, friend or family member. At some point in your previous incarnation, you likely let someone down and caused significant hurt with these behaviors and your lack of self-control.

The key to making amends in this life is to understand the value of self-control and to apply it to your life. This can be done through a variety of means, but structure is important. You still might have residual feelings of a need for freedom, maybe even at the expense of others, but in this life you need to realize that you can maintain a level of freedom while exercising self-control and behaving responsibly towards yourself and others. As counterintuitive as it may sound, having structure in your life is one way to gain control and fully utilize your personal freedom. Always keep in mind how your actions, even those that you think only involve you, truly affect others. Also, learn to be flexible. Being flexible is not the same as being rash or impulsive. It does not mean that if things do not go your way you should simply abandon the cause and head off in another direction by yourself. Instead, learn to take your challenges and sculpt your life into what you want it to be. Realize that this will take work, and more than likely, the help of others. In order to receive the help that you require in this life, you need to be someone who is trustworthy and dependable. Be someone who can be trusted, and focus on the needs of others before behaving impulsively or selfishly.

Sixteen

The energy associated with the karmic debt number sixteen can be viewed as somewhat explosive. This energy indicates a previous incarnation in which you may have misused or abused those who were in close relationships to you. You may have had anger or control issues which caused great harm, either physical or emotional, to others. The karmic number sixteen could be affecting your current life by making you feel as though there is an underlying current where you might explode or lose control. Others can sense this and might have difficulty trusting you completely. Another way that your past incarnations might be affecting your current life is that you may become a bit of an emotional recluse. The residual energy of your past life might still be hanging around, leaving you guarded, or it could be that your soul recognizes the pain that it has caused, so in an attempt at self-preservation, you turn inward and have difficulty connecting with other people.

If you carry the karmic debt number sixteen, you will want to make an effort to be more open and communicative with those in your life. Learn how to listen to understand rather than just to react. Realize that there is an ebb and flow to the energy of your ego and that this is a natural pattern of life. You do not always need to be the one at the top, and you should take care to open yourself up to the energy of others rather than shutting yourself off because you think that their energy could not possibly serve you any purpose. Making amends with the number sixteen is about opening yourself up to a more loving and forgiving energy. It is about having patience and being an equal in your personal relationships, rather than feeling the need to control them.

Nineteen

If you have the number nineteen as your karmic debt number, you can be sure that in a past incarnation you were a bully, or possibly materialistic and greedy. You likely took what you wanted without regard for other people. The key words associated with the karmic debt number nineteen are selfish, egotistical, narcissistic, self-important and self-involved.

Like many bullies and sybarites, you likely also suffered from an underlying lack of self-confidence or self-worth. You may have purposely hurt others or sought comfort from excess as a way of coping with your hurt. There may be a lot here that you have to atone for, depending upon the severity of your karmic load. However, amending the energy of the karmic number nineteen can be an incredibly rewarding growth experience. You now have the opportunity to serve as a leader and as an example. You should use this energy to help others reach their potential, while being kind and accepting. This is your chance to realize that material possessions are not what satisfies the spirit. Your past experience has given you great insight; now you need to share it with others, while being humble enough to know that this is not about you, but rather about them. You are not all-knowing, and you are no more important than anyone else, but you have been given the gift of insight that many others do not have. Share this selflessly, while admitting to yourself and others that while no one of us has all the answers, when we treat each other with respect and as equals, we evolve further in this lifetime.

Karmic Lesson Numbers

Karmic lessons are those things that we didn't quite get last time around (or the time before that, if you happen to have a particularly stubborn soul!). These are not wrongdoings or mistakes like the karmic debt numbers, but rather things that your soul needs to work on in this lifetime, or things that you need to learn. To calculate karmic lesson numbers, you look at the numbers that are missing from your name. I will go into an example in a bit, but I like to point this out early to make the connection between the numbers that are missing from your name and the lessons that are missing from your soul's life path. The numbers are not there because you have not yet passed through the learning experiences to earn those numbers. Recognizing these numbers and acknowledging their importance will benefit you in this life and any future incarnations.

Finding your karmic lesson number(s) is simple; it just involves looking at the alphanumeric chart in a different way. Rather than looking for the numbers that are represented and adding them together, we are looking for what is not there at all. For reference, here is the chart once again:

1	2	3	4	5	6	7	8	9
A	B	C	D	E	F	G	H	I
J	K	L	M	N	O	P	Q	R
S	T	U	V	W	X	Y	Z	.

You want to consider your entire birth name when looking for karmic lesson numbers. In this example, we will use the name Ellen Mary Smith.

First, we want to assign a numeric energy to each letter.

- E (5) L (3) L (3) E (5) N (5): The numbers 3 and 5 are represented.
- M (4) A (1) R (9) Y (7): The numbers 1, 4, 7 and 9 are represented.
- S (1) M (4) I (9) T (2) H (8): The numbers 1, 2, 4, 8 and 9 are represented.

So, in the name Ellen Mary Smith, we have the numbers 1, 2, 3, 4, 5, 7, 8 and 9 represented at least once. The only number that is missing is 6. This means that someone with the birth name of Mary Ellen Smith has a karmic lesson number of 6. She should pay close attention to the karmic energy associated with that number and take opportunities for learning and growth as they present themselves.

Each number has its own energy and meaning, but sometimes, especially when you are new to the science of numerology, understanding how that energy fits into each category can be overwhelming. To assist you in understanding the meaning of the numbers in karmic lessons, you can use this quick bullet list as a bit of a cheat sheet.

- Karmic Lesson Number 1: Self-sufficiency, independence, learning to trust yourself and your personal power
- Karmic Lesson Number 2: Community, unity, learning to support and encourage others, being part of something larger than yourself
- Karmic Lesson Number 3: Speaking your mind, articulation, trusting your creative instincts, learning to communicate effectively
- Karmic Lesson Number 4: Becoming grounded, practicality, letting go of wispy dreams in place of something solid and fruitful
- Karmic Lesson Number 5: Letting go of control, accepting change, learning to embrace the positive that comes with change
- Karmic Lesson Number 6: Personal responsibility, maturity, accountability, stepping up and doing what needs to be done, strengthening a sense of duty
- Karmic Lesson Number 7: Intellectual pursuits, acquiring knowledge, trusting your own thinking and reasoning skills, critical observation
- Karmic Lesson Number 8: Being driven, finding your passion and aspiring to your full potential, letting go of tendencies of laziness and procrastination
- Karmic Lesson Number 9: Strengthening your bond with others, acting with the best interests of others in mind, empathy, charity, acceptance

The Meaning of the Numbers

Numbers One through Nine: The Foundation of Numerology

In numerology, it is the single-digit numbers, one through nine, that form the foundation of the science and provide us with unique insight based upon their individual traits and characteristics. Within each of these numbers, there is a unique personality, not much different from what we think of as the human personality. Each of these numbers carries with it strengths, weaknesses, beauty, and sometimes a little quirkiness. Each number is truly an individual with its own personality. The first step in understanding numerology and how numbers affect our lives is developing a solid foundation for understanding these nine numbers.

As you are becoming acquainted with these numbers, keep in mind that numerology is part science and part intuition. Each number has a fixed set of qualities. These are based upon the vibrations of the number and do not change. However, how they react in certain categories or situations is open to some intuitive interpretation. The vibrations of the numbers can act singularly or interact among each other, creating a unique vibration field. These are the subtleties of numerology, and learning and attuning yourself to this all begins with understanding the foundation numbers.

As we go through and describe each of the vibrational energies associated with these numbers, you will find that there are positive and negative traits listed. Keep in mind that negative does not necessarily equal bad. Rather, think of it as the positive and negative energy of a battery, or the opposite poles of a magnet. Both are necessary; the key is to learn how to work with each effectively. Positive and negative must coexist with one another constructively.

One

Key words and traits: individual, determined, warrior, pragmatic, creator, leader, primal, beginnings

Of the foundational single-digit numbers, it is one that holds the significant responsibility of being the base, the force from which all the other numbers evolve and grow. There is some misconception about whether one or zero is the starting point of all the other numbers. When considering this, remember that zero is actually nothingness, and therefore nothing can grow from it unless a single seed is planted. For the purposes of numerology, we view the number one as that seed, the starting point from which all things spring forth.

The fact that number one gives birth to all the other numbers means that this number carries with it a sense of arrogance and self-importance. I like to think of the number one as having a parental energy, and what is done with this energy can greatly influence the outcome. For example, some parental figures are very authoritative, aggressive and controlling, while other parental figures are loyal and hardworking, with the best interests of all in their hearts. This is the dichotomy of the number one: a constant struggle between authority and spiritually significant big-picture perspective.

When the number one sets its sights on something, it knows no limits in terms of achieving its goals. There is no such thing as limited potential, and sometimes this philosophy can result in what can be viewed as aggressive energy. For the pure-hearted number one, the intent is building the necessary energy to get things done, check items off the list and move on to the next task. This number recognizes that sometimes aggressive energy is needed to turn dreams and goals into reality. This results in a very straightforward, results-driven personality.

Sometimes, the vibrational energy of one is misunderstood. To put the energy of this number in perspective, we should start by looking at the innate energy of the universe and nature. Everything starts from one. One seed, one raindrop, one cosmic interaction. There is an intense primal energy and force that is behind this number, because that is what is required for creation. Sometimes we view this primal energy as beautiful, and other times we view it as destructive. However, it is important to keep in mind that sometimes destruction is necessary in order for new growth to spring forth. The number one cannot discriminate; it simply knows what needs to be done for progress and growth and understands that sometimes this involves destruction and loss along the way. If you attempt to manipulate or control the vibrational energy of the number one, you are essentially interfering with the necessary processes of nature, and for that, there are almost always negative consequences. For this reason, it is important to understand that working with this energy sometimes requires a great deal of acceptance and surrender.

Positive Traits of Number One Energy
- Courageous
- Determined
- Responsible
- Honorable
- Loyal
- Protective
- Hardworking

Negative Traits of Number One Energy
- Confrontational
- Jealous
- Envious
- Stubborn

- Impatient
- Intimidating

One as a Life Path Number

If the number one is your life path number, then you are a true innovator. You have an eye for spotting the next big thing on the horizon and know how to turn any dream into a reality. The one life path knows no bounds when it comes to taking the right and appropriate action. This can be a good thing, since one is not only strong-willed, but generally against injustice of any type. However, whether you are looking at yourself or another, it is important to recognize that sometimes a one carries an attitude that their particular way of doing things is the *only* way. You should therefore be prepared for strong opposition should you come up against this energy. Ones are also easily bored and begin looking for the next challenge as soon as it becomes evident that success in one venture has been, or will be, achieved. This is great for business pursuits, but not so great when it comes to interpersonal relationships.

One as a Destiny Number

When the destiny number is one, it often represents the beginning of some type of a new cycle. This could be the first incarnation of life, or a fresh beginning in spiritual growth or path. This is exciting and can be viewed as a clean slate. As always when starting something new, there is often a degree of naïveté and arrogance that accompanies this new adventure. Be wary of this false sense of omniscience and invulnerability.

When one is the destiny number, the person is starting from scratch in some area of their development and growth. This means that the one might need to be guided and given advice regarding patience, acceptance and commitment. Although they might not always be receptive to this advice, they do in fact need to hear it. The one is an opportunist with intense drive. This can lead to a sense of restlessness when it comes to employment, relationships and home life. This is an example of why it is so important for the one to work on developing the fine nuances of appreciation for things that take time and nurturing to fully thrive. Being so result driven, the one likes to see results immediately and may feel that something that does not provide instant gratification is not worth their time and energy. This is true for matters both practical and spiritual, since those with the destiny number one are more likely to question the significance of spiritual matters that do not provide concrete proof or immediate results.

One as a Soul Number

When one is present as the soul number, it indicates someone who prefers to be in control in all aspects of life. This can bring both reward and unpleasantness, depending upon how this energy is utilized. One as a soul number is good for careers that require ambition and independence. Expect the soul number one to constantly be on the go, seeking adventure and taking risks for the sake of achievement and status. Soul number ones like to be rewarded and recognized for their efforts. For this reason, those with one as a soul number may be drawn to careers where recognition is standard, such as the military, or careers where one is "chosen," or elected, to lead based on their personality, drive and skill set. Ones are perfect in life paths that require a certain fire of creativity to effectively problem-solve. They are capable of seeing solutions to life's problems that others may not be able to see, because as ones, their vision is clear and unobstructed by past experiences.

Having a soul number of one brings with it an air of superiority, and light shines brightly within them. It is difficult not to be attracted to this innate drive and self-confidence. As a one, it is important to work on acknowledging that we all have a place in this world and that each of us has energy that vibrates on a different level. No one energy is more significant than another, and therefore it is important not to judge or act to harshly towards others, especially when their unique situation is one that you have no prior experience in. It is fine to be able to see solutions that those closest to the situation cannot see. It is another thing to expect those solutions to be accepted without being able to personally relate on any level. Being overly critical or contrary to authority can be a weakness for the soul number one that can hamper their success and development throughout life.

One as a Personality Number

One personalities are brilliant. They unite both male and female tendencies into a natural balance that is magnetic and attractive. They also exude great self-confidence, which tends to draw others into their circle. With the personality number one, it is important to find balance. As the birthplace of all other vibrational numbers, one naturally attracts others in and likes to be the center of attention. When combined with other one personalities, or others who understand how to work with the one energy, the result is nothing short of brilliant. The issue comes when there are power struggles or lack of foresight and planning that throw a one off track. However, when it comes to minor inconveniences (some of which other personality numbers would consider "major"), the one simple stands up, brushes off and moves on without much thought at all.

Personalities of one take great pride in their achievements, and there is not much that they can't do once they set their minds to it. They make great partners in life and business if you respect their need for authority and the fact that they may move on to new adventures before you are emotionally ready for them to. Even though the number one is an energy of birth and unity, it is also an energy of singularity and loneliness. The one personality requires both elements to feel balanced. With that in mind, the one personality strives to act in fairness and justice, for acting otherwise might lead to a negative reputation which would be considered a wound to their pride.

Two

Key Words and Traits: Gentle Leadership, Guidance, Nurturing, Dichotomy, Balance, Harmony, Inner Conflict

Of all the numbers, two expresses the most feminine energy. We can view the number two as a balance to the masculine, forward energy of the number one. Two is gentle, forgiving and compassionate, but also has an underlying strength. This can be seen in the way that the number two bends with its curves, almost as if it is someone on their knees, bent forward. What is present, but also might not be seen immediately, is the weight that bears down on the number two, causing the slight curvature. However, notice that while bowed, the two does not break, but instead supports with steadfast strength.

The number two is also one of compromise. It is the bridge between the aggressive energy of the number one and the more mature energies of the later numbers. Two is not a number of confrontation, but instead a number of peacemaking. It is important not to mistake this energy for being a pushover or over-accommodating. Two has a strong sense of self and morality, and will not sit back and accept abuse or misuse of any sort. There is only so much that a two can hold before that slight bend might turn into a complete break. When pushed, the number two will exhibit warrior-like qualities that are normally kept below the surface to prevent this from happening.

There is a flowing, sensual energy to the number two. The two is able to understand multiple viewpoints and perspectives, which makes this number a good teacher or leader. There is a gentleness to these leadership qualities that people are naturally attracted to and respect. The two knows how to use these energies to its advantage, and while not being purposefully deceptive, knows how to appeal to different personality types in order to promote an agenda. If you have been influenced by a two, chances are you will not recognize it, except in hindsight. The two persuades you into believing that it was your idea in the first place. This flowing energy of two also means that there are often creative and artistic qualities at play. This could be in the form of the arts, but the number two is likely to find ways of being creative and expressive no matter what they are doing. The two is intuitive and loyal, which in proper balance are viewed as positive qualities. However, when out of balance, these traits can manifest themselves in the form of jealousy and demanding neediness.

Positive Traits of Number Two Energy
- Giving
- Sharing
- Compassionate
- Empathetic
- Counseling
- Protective

Negative Traits of Number Two Energy
- Jealous
- Possessive
- Shy
- Overly Emotional
- Unbalanced
- Low Self Esteem

Two as a Life Path Number

If two is your life path number, your purpose is to be someone who blazes trails, but with a gentle flame that warms but never burns. You are a visionary, but also know that acting the part of the bull and charging your way through scenarios without regard to your surroundings is no way to accomplish your goals. Instead, you rely on your intuition and your ability to truly listen to others. You pay attention to details and have an incredible memory. This serves you well, as you intuitively use what you know about someone or a situation to help mold the path that it will take. This is not considered manipulation, but rather such an innate understanding of the situation that you intuitively know what it needs, often when others are not yet able to see it.

A key point for the number two as a life path number is routine. As a two, you need structure; otherwise, you begin to feel off-balance. The two as a life path is prone to becoming overly emotional or overstressed when routine and structure are broken. The two does its best not to let others see this, and might even deny these emotions to itself, so they often simmer below the surface until they reach the boiling point and overflow. From someone else's perspective, this can seem like it came out of nowhere, giving the two an air of emotional instability. In fact, it is one of the most level-headed numbers—as long as there is routine and organization.

If two is your life path number, it is important to remember to keep things in perspective and to treat yourself with the same grace and forgiveness that you extend to others. This can be difficult for your perfectionist personality, but not allowing yourself this will expose you to extremes of emotion and frustration that are not only uncomfortable but will also keep you from reaching your full and true potential.

Two as a Destiny Number

Two as a destiny number is a symbol of growth and potential. The two is more mature than the one, but there is still plenty of opportunity ahead for it. The two has the advantage of being able to view this potential from a more experienced and mature perspective. If two is your destiny number, be prepared for opportunities for growth on all levels to present themselves. You should also be aware of some of the words associated with the number two, such as "double" or "twice." You might have to work twice as hard at some points to reach your goals, or you may have to go through the process of working through some challenges a second time before everything finds its natural rhythm and falls into place.

The destiny number of two has a very strong connection to the home. It thrives on a sense of security and all being well and happy on the home front. If you have two as a destiny number and are feeling as though your home life is chaotic or not as warm and welcoming as you would like it to be, some introspection might be in order to bring about a sense of peace and contentment. Two as a destiny number tends to be very hard on itself. This can lead to self-depreciation and all the negative emotions that come with it. As the person with two as a destiny number, these are difficult emotions to cope with and attempt to grow through. Additionally, the underlying lack of self-worth can make other people uncomfortable, and you may have difficulty maintaining significant relationships and creating a home with other people. The solution to this is to look inside yourself and learn to appreciate and value your individual beauty and worth. Combine this with activities that help you see natural beauty and growth. You might be drawn to peaceful natural environments, or activities such as gardening that allow you to immerse yourself in the natural process and witness the order and beauty of nature.

Two as a Soul Number

Two is one of the easiest numbers to visualize, and if you take a few minutes to meditate on its energy, you can open yourself up to the possibilities of two as a soul number. Think for a moment

85

about the importance of two in our physical existence. It takes two people to create a life. We have an innate human instinct to find someone who we feel complements us to the point where the two distinct people, who are complete on their own, blend together to create a union of one. The philosophy of yin and yang involves two opposite but complementary energies; we seek out second opinions; we have inner contradictions involving two opposing aspects of ourselves.

Two as a soul number needs harmony, symmetry and balance. Anything that unbalances this will be uncomfortable to two. Twos understand the value of working as a team. They know that sometimes they are the ones who need to step forward and be in the spotlight, although this is not their natural place, and they know that the roles behind the scenes are often the most important and influential. Two understands this exchange and the natural flow of energy that accompanies it. People with the soul number of two have an ability to make anyone feel comfortable and welcome.

If there is a downside to having two as a soul number, it is that this energy tends to become easily discouraged. When things become too difficult, especially if this difficulty involves conflict with others, the soul number two is compelled to back down, even if there is value in seeing the fight through. For this reason, soul number two is hesitant to build relationships, either personal or business, with people who have an aggressive, demanding or bully-like energy about them. This is a protective measure on their part, as their accommodating nature might be viewed as a weak spot for someone looking to take advantage. However, taking the time to get to know someone and understand their energy is sometimes more productive and beneficial than simply running away from it.

Two as a Personality Number

The personality number of two is strongly connected to partnership and cooperation, which is in contrast to the singular energy of the number one. Two personalities strive for companionship and building strong relationships. The feminine energy associated with the personality number two brings with it nurturing tendencies, giving a strong "mama-bear" energy to the two personalities. This person may seem to go with the flow—until someone or something threatens someone they love and care about, at which point you might be surprised at the drastic change of demeanor of this personality type.

Along with that feminine, mama-bear energy, comes the natural ability to see when someone is hurting, or in need of advice. The advice that comes from the number two personality is almost always sound, reasonable and given with the best of intentions. This personality number has highly developed intuition and a great capacity for showing empathy. Two personalities are great at giving counsel, which makes them people that you want on your side.

The duality of the two personality also means that they might experience struggles between opposing forces. For example, the strong desire to hold others close and form relationships is at odds with a naturally self-protective nature that makes twos slow to warm up to new people and build relationships. Another example is the seemingly endless ability to build other people up while quietly tearing themselves down. Two personalities might find themselves in intimate battles between opposing sides of themselves. The two personality is also spiritually inclined and typically likes to spend time appreciating the beauty of nature. When a two personality is in touch with these aspects of itself, it will find it easier to balance the opposing forces within.

Three

Key Words and Traits: Energy, Enthusiasm for Life, Extroversion, Creativity, Optimism

We have talked about the masculine energy of the number one and the feminine energy of the number two. Those two numbers both contradict and complement each other. If we think of this combination of masculine and feminine energy as the starting point for all other numbers, then it is logical to think of the number one and the number two as "parents." Who is the first child of this coupling? The number three.

Three is a combination of the attributes of the number one and the number two. It has a strong, active energy, but the number three is also drawn to creativity and fluidity. The three has a strong personality, and is a charming extrovert, but the three also has a side that is quieter, more reflective and emotional. People with threes in their charts are generally well liked by many, as their dual nature and outgoing attitude makes them especially easy to get along with.

The key to learning to navigate the strengths and challenges of having the number three in your chart is to recognize that this number, although talented and well-liked, is still a bit immature. The three still has an incredible amount of growth to go through, which can be difficult for them because three has a tendency to procrastinate and be slow to take personal responsibility. The three may struggle in areas of academics and business, not because it is not capable, but because it isn't willing, or is simply too distracted. The three is a bit of a daydreamer and will almost always prefer to be doing something creative, something social, or just plain enjoying life rather than drudging through the less-than-enjoyable activities. It isn't that three is lazy; it is that three has not yet learned and developed perseverance, or a high regard for structure and organization. Threes can sometimes seem as though they are lacking in the morality department. Again, this is not a representation of the potential that is within them, but rather a symptom of their need for guidance and support in order to grow.

If you have a three in your chart, you may find that challenges are put in front of you that require commitment and discipline— usually when you are least in the mood to participate. For your own wellbeing, make structuring your personal environment a top priority. Threes are the type of people who love the idea of whirlwind world travel, or buying an RV to live and travel in as a way of life. These aren't bad things, but they will not help you to develop the foundation that is needed to succeed and to feel true happiness and fulfillment. Instead, place yourself in an environment with a stable foundation, where you will have the support and discipline to develop your strengths and talents. The three has an innate understanding of cycles of life; it simply needs to learn how to apply this knowledge to its own life as well.

Positive Traits of Number Three Energy
- Social
- Friendly
- Loyal
- Energetic
- Charismatic

Negative Traits of Number Three Energy
- Easily Bored
- Disenchanted
- Moody
- Fickle
- Lack of Discipline

Three as a Life Path Number

Those with the life path number of three take joy in living life to its fullest and making the most of every experience. They are people who have a positive outlook on life and tend to look for the best in any situation. Threes have an aura of charisma and charm. Combined with their positive outlook, this means that they have a magnetic personality that others are often immediately drawn to. A life path of three, when in balance, has no shortage of friends or opportunities to engage socially. When the three respects and values these relationships, they will always get the support that they need, provided that they make their needs known.

Because the three is so outgoing and sharing, it tends to feel that its openness should be returned without question. When it isn't, or when things don't go their way, they can have a tendency toward moodiness and clouds of darkness that contradict their typical nature. Part of this is the fact that three, while intuitive, doesn't always have the patience to understand that we are all working at different levels and that we all have subtle nuances to our personalities. We each express ourselves differently, and while the three is one of the most expressive numbers, it can have a hard time understanding when others do not share that same energy.

The life path number of three indicates that you are well suited for careers that require teamwork, interaction and connection. Because you can so easily reach out to others, you might find that you are drawn to careers that involve a lot of networking, meeting new clients and experiencing different cultures. Because three is creative and likes a constant flow of change and excitement, settling down into one stable life path can be difficult for them. Unfortunately, this distraction can leave those with the life path of three prone to financial difficulties and unstable employment. When the three is on target, the three is brilliant. However, when the three is feeling disenchanted and bored, three energy often causes frustration and resentment in others.

If you have three as a life path number, follow your dream and never lose sight of your optimistic and explorative nature. Remember, however, that the mundane parts of life are necessary and integral for balance. You cannot live a one-sided life and expect positive results. A major goal for you is to learn how to control your zest for life and energy so it can be guided to do good and fulfill you on a spiritual level.

Three as a Destiny Number

With three as a destiny number, your eccentric nature is both a blessing and a curse. People are naturally drawn to you, but they can feel a little overstimulated when you never seem to come back down to earth. Throughout your life, you will find that people want to develop significant relationships with you, that people want your creative talents to be a part of their team. However, the demands of these relationships are going to stretch your boundaries of personal freedom. This is a major life lesson for you: learning how not to lose yourself, while not losing relationships and opportunities.

Coming to terms with this requires a combination of compromise and sticking up for yourself. Too many times people, especially those with strong threes in their chart, are made to feel like their eccentric nature and lack of appreciation for the mundane are negative characteristics that must be eradicated. I strongly disagree with this. These are beautiful qualities in the destiny number three—if you learn how to balance them with the reality of life. This is where you will need to compromise, but never to the point that you entirely lose yourself. Instead, learn how to better focus your energy and accept that personal responsibility is real and important.

Those with the destiny number of three are open, loyal, and at times naïve. The fact that you easily open yourself up to so many others means that your odds of getting hurt are increased. Stay open, but also learn that a little self-protection is an important quality to have.

Three as a Soul Number

One of your personal mottos should be "You can please some of the people some of the time, but none of the people all of the time." You have a genuinely good spirit, and your energy and enthusiasm about life is contagious. You like to make other people feel good, and you enjoy lifting them up and helping them to see all the beauty in life that you see every day. These are great qualities, but they might not always be appreciated, at least not to the degree that you think they should be. This has the potential to leave you feeling undervalued and deflated. With three as a soul number, a major lesson for you is to realize that you do not have the ability to control other people's happiness. You can try, but some people will resist. Let this go; that is part of their soul's journey and not yours.

With exuberance comes a heightened energy that can be developed into something more significant in the spiritual or metaphysical realm. It might take you some time to get there, since you tend to lack discipline and focus, but when you are ready, these are doors that will be open for you.

Three as a Personality Number

Three is a very strong personality number. Think for a moment about all the threes that occur in our lives: Past, Present, Future; Body, Mind, Soul; Mother, Father, Child; Childhood, Adolescence, Adulthood; Birth, Life, Death; Liquid, Solid, Gas; Food, Water, Air. The number three is a significant influence in all our lives, but even more so for those with the number three as their personality number. You will find that you feel most peaceful, most fulfilled, when the energy of three is working for you. This could be a balance between home, work and play. It could be that you are one of three close friends who complement each other. We tend to think of two as being the number of symmetry, but three can be equally balancing, which is something that is important for a three to achieve in their lifetime.

As a personality number three, you might find that you are the great balancer among your friends or coworkers. Think of yourself in the middle, standing between two extremes. Three's energy tends to be more active, but the sensitive intuition of three also recognizes the necessity of stillness. You have a natural ability to stand between two opposing forces and blend them into one constructive force.

You will find that your greatest happiness comes from social environments where you have the opportunity to spread your charm and make others happy. Do not deny yourself these pleasures, but use this turn in life to learn how to harness this energy and use it towards something that fulfills you on an even deeper level. We all have something that drives us, something that will excite us even through the drudgery. This is your calling, to find that thing. When you are balanced, when the power of three is working strongly within you, you will find that you are capable of great and beautiful things.

Four

Key Words and Traits: Stability, Dedication, Determination, Goals, Dependability, Hard Work

I always find it interesting to write each of the numbers and notice how they are constructed, and then look at the descriptions for each of the numbers and discover how they are similar in so many ways. I want to take a minute here and go back through the three previous numbers as an example. The one is made of a singular strong line. It is masculine, forceful, almost like an exclamation point, but it seems a little underdeveloped. Then we look at the two, which while bending and bowing, also has an incredibly strong foundation that will not let it fold completely under. The two is gentler, more feminine than the one. Next, we come to the number three, with its curves that seem to mimic a bouncing rubber ball, which is not unlike the fun, spirited energy of three. Now, we come to the number four, and when we look at it, we can see straight lines, sharp corners and rigid construction. This, in a nutshell, describes the number four energy.

The number four tends to work in straight lines. It knows what it wants and how to get it. Planning and organization are important to the number four, and it does not take shortcuts or try to take the easy way out. You can count on those with fours in their charts to be predictable, loyal, hardworking and productive. In sharp contrast to the energy of number three, the four is not a social butterfly; in fact, four would much prefer a quiet night in. Some might view this type of laid-back, quiet steadfastness as boring; however, once you get to know the number four, you will see that he has plenty of character. He simply does not like to draw attention to himself.

You can probably deduce from the description so far that those with the number four in their chart are good workers, often viewed as the best employees. They go above and beyond when necessary, but are smart about how they spend their energy. You will likely find fours in leadership roles or other positions that required diligence and determination to achieve. Be sure that when a four is in power, it is not the result of a lofty goal that came to life with the help of luck and the right circumstances. The four gets to where they are through planning, organization and effort. Fours can easily recognize when something is out of reach, and therefore you won't likely find a four trying fruitlessly to achieve the unattainable.

Fours are natural builders. They are good with lines, numbers and puzzles. While we can apply this to trades and hobbies, we can also apply this to life in general. Fours understand that relationships and achieving goals require a strong foundation. Many people with the number four in their charts rely on religious belief and structure to form part of that foundation. Fours like answers, so they don't like any philosophy that seems a little wispy. They are drawn to traditional religions more than fluid spirituality.

The very traits that make four strong are the same ones that can contribute to its downfall. Their own strict doctrine can leave them unyielding and uncompromising. Their emphasis on reliability and structure can mean that they do not always open themselves up to new and enjoyable experiences. Some might say that a four is too strict, too demanding and too dull. The fact that four's ego can be easily bruised by any type of negative word aimed at its reputation only compounds these issues. Just like with all the other numbers, balance is the key. When in balance, the fours are the ones who can rebuild and recreate the world if they put their minds to it.

Positive Traits of Number Four Energy
- Dependable
- Loyal
- Goal Oriented
- Successful
- Hardworking
- Honest
- Straightforward

Negative Traits of Number Four Energy
- Harsh
- Judgmental
- Self-Depreciating
- Serious to a fault
- Tunnel Vision
- Introverted

Four as a Life Path Number

If four is your life path number, you can rest assured that success is in the cards for you; it is unavoidable. Your determination and work ethic will serve you well. It is important to note that some fours will work too hard, to the point that their hard work is taken advantage of and their efforts are overlooked. This is not typically the case, although it can occur if your other energies are out of balance. In general, the life path number four is too intelligent to let this happen. They know how to work smartly, without wasting personal resources.

One of the key points for people with the life path number of four is that while many others see work, chores, studies, as things that must be done, fours see them as enjoyable. Fours love to learn, they love to know how things work, and they love results.

The downside of having a life path number of four is that it can be easy for you to work too much, simply because that is what you know how to do best. You can feel lost and purposeless when there is no work to do. This will only be exaggerated by the fact that people will naturally come to you when something needs to be done, because they know they can trust you to do the job. Unfortunately, this does nothing to help you achieve balance. Meditation is one way to help yourself learn how to relax; however, you may be better suited for yoga, because then you will at least feel like you are doing something while you are learning to be at peace with not constantly running through your to-do list!

Four as a Destiny Number

The word destiny has an air of mystique about it, implying that the future will unfold in a magical way. This is not how a four views destiny. A four views destiny as something that is planned for, something whose outcome is a result of thought and organization. However, the four does not typically view destiny as fluid, because once their mind is made up about something, there is no turning back. Fours can appreciate the go-with-the-flow nature of other numbers, but will likely clash with them if they try too hard to impose that nature.

Don't be inclined to believe that the four, with all its structure and rigidness, is meant to be alone. The truth is quite the contrary. People with four as a destiny number are loyal and dependable. These are attractive qualities when looking for a friend or romantic partner. However, the things that the four brings to the relationship are the very things that they will look for in return. Fours choose quality over quantity every time, and if you don't measure up, don't plan on being able to stick around. The four can encounter a great deal of hurt and heartache as it learns how to navigate personal relationships and how to spot those that are true and worthy of their time.

Four as a Soul Number

Four is the number of discipline. Its lines are purposeful and decisive. This structure and need for organization makes up the very core of who you are. While these are admirable qualities, the four can have a difficult time accepting anything else from others.

If you have four as a soul number, one of your main lessons is to learn how to satisfy your inner need for stability, structure and security while at the same time learning not to impose this on others who do not live their lives the same way. A life lived on a whim, or with less organization than your own, might not make any sense to you, but that doesn't mean that they are less than you or not worthy of your respect. With the soul number of four, the goal is to learn how to open your mind and heart. You are well respected and trusted; make sure that you use those gifts for the good of others rather than tearing them down with your judgment.

Four as a Personality Number

With the number three, we were able to look at how some of the most powerful influences in life come with the number three. We can do something similar with the number four in regard to strength and stability. A car has four wheels; a chair has four legs; there are four cardinal directions; a room has four corners; there are four seasons. All of these things bring to mind stability, balance and completion. You can easily divide almost anything into four quarters and have nice, neat little pockets of organization, just as the four prefers.

As a personality, all this stability and security might sound boring, and to be honest, to some people it might be. But as a four, you already know that you don't mesh well with everyone, and that is just fine. You are actually most content with your inner circle of friends and family, the people who already get you and know that there is a certain magic within your personality. You are honest, you are trustworthy, and your dry sense of humor can often be the life of the party, although that is certainly not your intention.

With the personality number of four in this incarnation, the work you are doing is serious and will have long-lasting effects. This is not a playful life for you, although play is certainly encouraged. You just know that this time you need to get down to business. There is no time to waste on frivolous or superficial matters when you are putting in the work that will affect your future incarnations. You know that slow and steady wins the race, and you are not going to risk your chances at success by stopping off and being lazy along the way.

Five

Key Words and Traits: Outgoing, Adventurous, Risk Taker, Live in the Moment, Addiction

Five lies right in the middle of the nine single-digit numbers in numerology. With this type of placement, you can expect the five to keep you guessing. The number five displays qualities that are both rigid and fluid, masculine and feminine, and you can never be quite sure where the five is along those spectrums at any given moment, because five thrives on change.

Five is strong, independent, and also prone to boredom. Especially in youth and young adulthood, the five is a risk taker, and might have a difficult time settling down to one task, so don't expect a five to head straight into college from high school and be committed to a particular career track. Drawn-out studies and boring careers are the last thing on the mind of a young five. As the five matures, their more feminine energy comes into play and they are intuitively drawn to things that spark their passion. This is where you will find a five finally begin to consider commitment.

This same fiery, ever-changing energy of the five can make them difficult partners to settle down with until they are into middle adulthood. They can also be fickle with friends who don't understand their true nature. The explorative nature of the five does not intend to hurt anyone; it is just that their freely flowing energy is not understood by everyone. In fact, when a five finds their people, they are one of the most loyal numbers, and the least likely to betray a close relationship. The key to a five's heart is to not impose any limitations.

One of the strongest characteristics of the five is their adaptability. They can take anything that you throw at them and adjust easily to change. They are naturally smart, forward-thinking and charismatic. This is the type of energy that is capable of making great changes in the world when it is focused rather than allowed to run wild. People with strong fives in their charts stand strong in the middle, but their subtler energies can be easily influenced by the people in their lives. The masculine and feminine energy within the five can ebb and flow, depending upon the situation and who they have in their lives. Too much influence from either side can affect the five negatively. The strong control of the more masculine numbers fights against the nature of five, while the flowing energy of the feminine numbers can only exaggerate some of the five's less desirable qualities. For a number that strives for change and adventure, the five needs a surprising amount of balance.

One thing that a five always has to keep in mind is that there is more at stake than just today. Tomorrow will come, and what you do today will affect your future. It can be difficult for a five to give much thought to the future, and at times the actions of someone with this number in their chart can feel reckless, selfish and irresponsible. The five has a need for instant gratification, and can sometimes sacrifice too much to achieve it. For the five, it is important to learn how to achieve satisfaction without being self-destructive in the process.

Positive Traits of Number Five Energy
- Adventurous
- Adaptable
- Open-minded
- Trustworthy
- Social

Negative Traits of Number Five Energy
- Non-committal
- Flighty
- Bored

- Addictive Tendencies
- Irresponsible

Five as a Life Path Number

A life path number of five comes with a flair for adventure and experience. You tend to prefer the extreme side of the scale and live your life in full color. Nothing is ever just black and white for a five, nor is it grey. If five is your life path number, you find dogmatic structure boring, and there is nothing that you detest more than boredom. The five is arguably the most sensual of the numbers, in the sense that you seek to experience everything to the fullest extent possible. If you feel something, you feel it intensely. If you touch something, you feel every little fiber that others miss. When you see something, you look at it from a different perspective and notice every detail. When you love, it is with your whole heart, and when you have negative feelings towards someone, those are very intense too.

With the life path number five, one of your lessons is to learn how to get in touch with your more practical side. You might not believe that you have one, but you do. At some point, there will be responsibility placed in your hands, and you will need to bear the weight. When this happens, remember that stability isn't boring, especially when you can bring your own unique touches to the task at hand. You have seemingly boundless energy. Rather than frittering it away frivolously, why not focus it and use it on something that will give you a greater sense of satisfaction and personal pride? Your expanded vision means that you have the ability to see and experience things in this life that many others never open their eyes to. This is a gift that should not be wasted.

Five as a Destiny Number

Five as a destiny number can be summed up in the word "experience." You are in constant motion, moving effortlessly from one thing to the next. On one hand, this is good, because you are not bogged down with the emotional and physical baggage that keeps other numbers stagnant. However, constant movement can also cause distress in both your personal and professional lives. While you are loyal at heart, your actions can make you seem untrustworthy. You are someone with good intentions and a strong enough work ethic, and you *can* follow through; you just don't sit still long enough for many people to be able to recognize this about you.

As a five, you are charmed and can do anything that you put your mind to, so go ahead and focus your energy on your passions. Just make sure to keep it focused, or else everything that is within your grasp can slip away while you are distracted.

Five as a Soul Number

Your soul is one that craves freedom. With a soul number of five, you are likely drawn to travel and new experiences. There is no shyness or awkwardness about you, and you adapt to new situations with ease. It is important to recognize that you march to the beat of a different drummer, and that it is difficult for you to find others who keep up the same pace. You might find that accepting this is a lifelong challenge for you. Your energy is contagious; however, there is a need to respect the speed at which others move. If you do not accept that we each have our own rhythm and energy for life, then you will likely find yourself facing years of frustration and damaged relationships.

It is essential for you to find someone who can at least appreciate your explorative, curious and constantly moving energy. Partnering your energy with one that is dogmatic and restrictive can have serious consequences for your mental health. You cannot be boxed in, and will only feel comfortable settling down when you know that you still have freedom. People are strongly attracted to your charisma, and you might encounter those who want to be with you so much that they will attempt to hold you in too tightly. For you, it is important to avoid these relationships at all costs. Five as a soul number is very loyal by nature. The right partner will recognize that there is no need to restrain you, because once you have committed your heart, you will never stray, even if you are still constantly in motion and seeking new experiences.

With maturity, the soul number five will learn to appreciate the value of a slightly slower pace. You will never lose your sense of adventure, but you will come to learn that slowing down a little gives you more opportunity to fully take in all the experiences and allows you to see potential pitfalls before they swallow you up.

Five as a Personality Number

When you enter a crowded room and immediately find one person who sparkles and shines, chances are you are looking at someone with the personality number of five. Fives love interaction and activity, and if they are present, you can bet that there won't be a dull moment. They simply won't allow it to happen. Even when placed in situations that require a quieter, slower pace, the five personality has a way of breathing new and fresh life into the air. Fives despise boredom and monotony, and the combination of the two is a recipe for misery.

104

When you get entangled with a five, you should be prepared for a bumpy ride. The five does not believe in convention the way most of the other numbers do, so you will find them taking approaches that you never even dreamed possible. Sometimes, this works out magnificently, while other times, the lack of foresight results in a less desirable outcome. Boundaries are difficult for a five to envision, accept or create.

With all this whirlwind energy, the five still likes balance and harmony. This "middle child" of the numbers likes to be the peacemaker, and will naturally act as a mediator when conflict and divisions begin to occur. They are a great ally to have on your side because you can trust them to have a balanced perspective and to be truthful. In the five's world, things are constantly changing and shifting. They realize that honesty is a way of keeping things moving. When we are less than truthful, or tell people only what they want to hear, we risk stagnation, and the five recognizes this more than the other numbers.

Six

Key Words and Traits: Nurturing, Healing, Self-Sacrificing, Harmony, Maternal

As I mentioned, I like to look at the actual shape and configuration of each of the numbers as a clue to what they hold. This is an excellent way of learning how to use your intuition when it comes to numerology. Unlike people, who are not always what they seem, numbers are more transparent. When you look at the six, you can see that it resembles a woman with a full, heavy womb, on the verge of motherhood. The six embodies these maternal qualities and is the most compassionate and understanding of the numbers.

The six strives for harmony in her life. She is nurturing, loving, and has a gentle healing energy about her. Family, whether related by blood or by the heart, is at the top of the list of priorities for the number six. She thrives on feelings of belonging, intimacy and community. The energy of this number is essential in all types of organizational units, from the smallest family to the largest corporation.

As one can imagine, with such love and maternal instincts comes the potential to become overly involved, and this is perhaps the most noticeable character flaw for those with the number six in their charts. This can manifest itself as appearing needy, meddling, or losing too much of yourself to the energy of others. The six has a heart that is open and receptive, and she gives her love easily, without expecting too much in return.

Those with a strong presence of the number six in their charts are highly suited for careers that involve caring or nurturing on some level. Think of teachers, missionaries, veterinarians, and those in the healthcare field. The six is naturally drawn to those who are weak or frail, either physically or in spirit. While gentle and mild-mannered, the six has a fierce side that comes out when she senses injustice, irresponsibility or ill intent. The six is the quintessential mother bear with an energy that is a force to be reckoned with.

Positive Traits of Number Six Energy
- Giving
- Nurturing
- Loving
- Healing
- Protective

Negative Traits of Number Six Energy
- Self-depreciating
- Self-sacrificing to a fault
- Jealous
- Overbearing

Six as a Life Path Number

Those with the number six as a life path number have strong domestic ties. What happens in your own home is your number-one priority, and you will sacrifice nearly anything to make sure that those you love and care about are protected, loved and nurtured. Your eye is sharp, and you can tell instantly when something is out of place. Then you instantly try to rectify the situation in an attempt to bring back balance and harmony.

One area that those with the life path number six don't have such keen insight in is understanding the true nature of people. You have a tender heart, and you like to assume the best about people until they prove otherwise. This isn't a bad philosophy to have, except that it leaves you open to being hurt or taken advantage of. For the six, it is difficult to learn how to balance remaining open with retaining a sufficient amount of self-protection. If six is your life path number, practice being as vocal and forthcoming about your own needs as you would about the needs of others. You need to take care of yourself, so make a point of not neglecting your own personal, spiritual or emotional needs.

Challenges that come with having the number six as a life path number include realizing that while not everyone has the best of intentions, that does not mean that all of humanity is lost. As a six, you tend to hold onto the sting of being wronged, and for a time you will transpose that onto other people undeservingly. If the six in the group isn't happy, then chances are that no one is. This isn't fair to those around you, especially when they might not even understand the origins of your discontent. Secondly, you have a tendency to be too controlling. There is a balance between being true to your nature and respecting the personal boundaries of others.

Six as a Destiny Number

Do unto others as you want others to do unto you is the motto that best applies to the destiny number of six. With the energy associated with this number, balance is important to you. You don't like the scales to tip too much in either direction, so you strive to keep your environment as harmonious as possible, which can mean expending quite a bit of energy on the affairs of others. People seek you out for advice, and you readily give it. You are a magnet for those in need of counsel and nurturing.

Those with six in the destiny number category typically feel strongly connected to everything spiritual. They believe in a greater good, and feel connected to the universal energies. This is also a number associated with strong emotions. While you are taking the time to soothe and comfort others, take care not to neglect your own personal wellbeing. Do not hold everything in. Yell it out instead of swallowing it down. You need to do things like this to clear the energy within you and around you.

Six as a Soul Number

When six is your soul number, you crave stability and security, and you do not react well when either of those things is compromised. Your typically loving and generous nature will quickly shift to one that is controlling and intrusive in an attempt to regain the harmony and balance that you require. This can make some interpersonal relationships difficult, and you may have a hard time understanding why this is so. You are someone who gives freely, and you might feel that it's only fair that everyone goes along with you because of how much you give to others. Think of the overbearing mother-in-law with the best of intentions. She is loved and appreciated, but sometimes, she just goes too far. To salvage some of your relationships, you will need to learn that other people, even those closest to you, are entitled to their personal boundaries.

Six as a Personality Number

To fully understand six as a personality number, all you need to do is take everything that you have read about the six so far and magnify it by about ten. The six symbolizes the energy of unselfish and unconditional love. The six is nurturing, emotional, protective, and healing. The six is the first one to show up when someone is in need, and they will continue to give of themselves for as long as necessary.

For six, taking care of others is just the way of nature. While this number is emotional and nurturing, the six will take care of someone using whatever means they have. For some sixes, this might mean providing financially for someone who is having difficulty standing on their own feet. This energy can also come in the form of protectiveness, and while I have highlighted the mother bear energy, mostly because six energy has strong female characteristics, a male with six as a personality number can be strongly protective. Anyone who tries to cross a line with him should be prepared for a major battle.

Because the six is so busy taking care of other people, self-neglect is often an issue, although a six will be the last one to recognize this. Unfortunately, sometimes the six is at risk of being taken advantage of. They are just too idealistic to see any negative potential, at least until they get hurt, at which point you can expect a six to enter a dark, downward spiral, at least temporarily.

Seven

Key Words and Traits: Intelligent, Knowledge, Curious, Spiritual, Seeker

I like to view the number seven as a person standing and looking around, maybe with their hand over their eyes to offer some shade from the sun. The number seven is the seeker of the group. They seek knowledge, they seek understanding, and they seek justice. There are few things that you can hide from a seven, for they seem to have the keys to uncovering all sorts of truths, even those that you would rather keep to yourself.

The seven spends so much time sitting back and observing the surroundings that at first you might think of them as an introvert. In some cases, they are, and are genuinely uncomfortable in social situations. On the other hand, a seven might just be waiting for the perfect time to join in on the party. To them, timing is everything. Those with sevens in their chart are often quiet and sometimes soft-spoken. This frequently leads people to misunderstand them. They can be seen as shy or lacking self-confidence. The truth is that the seven is very intelligent, and not just in a book smart way. The seven looks at the entire world and uses its knowledge to dream up all the possibilities. You might expect conventional ideas from seven, but that is not always what you will get.

If you are looking for an opinion, you can be sure that seven has one, whether it is popular or not. The seven lives in a world that is a blending of an unending quest for knowledge and a daydreamer's spirit. This is a combination that can lead to some interesting outcomes, so when you ask a seven for advice (or they give it anyway!), know that their ideas may be a little off-center. This doesn't mean that the seven gives bad advice; it is just that they are coming from a different perspective, one that sees a world that the rest of us don't envision quite so easily.

Sevens have unique, incredibly interesting personalities. If you love having conversations about an endless variety of topics, and have a taste for a dry sense of humor, then a seven is your true mate. However, any seven knows that they have a tendency become arrogant at times. Their quest for knowledge and unique understanding of the world leaves them a little calloused to other people's problems and issues. Unless you are someone the seven cares about deeply, don't expect them to become too involved in any of your personal drama. In fact, they despise it and can be quite sharp-tongued when their patience is tested.

Positive Traits of Number Seven Energy
- Inquisitive
- Visionary
- Unique
- Loyal
- Intelligent

Negative Traits of Number Seven Energy
- Isolated
- Judgmental
- Lost in thought
- Unfocused

Seven as a Life Path Number

Sevens are unique thinkers and visionaries. They have an unyielding curiosity and love a challenge. For the seven, it is not just about finding answers, but also understanding the "why." Where other people might put together a puzzle, the seven is examining the shapes and the intricate details of each piece. They strive for perfection and don't like making mistakes. When given a task, the seven will work on it until it is not only completed, but also perfect. This is great, except for when you need something done quickly. The seven does not really have a concept of time when knowledge and strategy are concerned, making it appear that the seven lives in its own little world.

In a sense, the seven *does* live in its own world. People with sevens as a life path number are not interested in acquiring friends just for the sake of having them. They can also be difficult to befriend, because they find the things that other people enjoy to be mundane and boring. A seven is not interested in shiny or pretty, but rather deep and intellectual. A downside of the seven is that they might not realize that something, or someone, can fall into both of those categories at the same time. A seven can be superficial in their own way.

If you have a seven as a life path number, you probably find more value in solitude than others. To you, a little alone time is necessary for personal growth. It is during these moments of quiet and solitude that you delve into more spiritual matters and begin a quest of self-discovery. Due to your naturally inquisitive nature, this quest may take you on many tangents and roads you never anticipated going down, but this doesn't surprise you. You already know that true knowledge and discovery requires discovering and exploring the unknown.

Seven as a Destiny Number

If lucky number seven is your destiny number, you will likely feel some spiritual intervention in your life. By this I mean that you will find yourself being pulled in certain directions when paying attention to your intuition, or through divine guidance in the form of dreams, psychic readings, etc. You are one who loves knowledge and needs to understand everything, and from this perspective it might seem like metaphysical and spiritual matters would not be your cup of tea because they are not concrete enough for you. However, you have an intense curiosity and an open mind, which leaves you quite perceptive to influential energies. This is also part of what gives you that visionary vibe.

With the destiny number seven, your mind needs to be active, so you are best suited for careers that give you a good degree of freedom to let you explore and investigate as you please. If you get tied down to a more traditional career, do not neglect your inner need for knowledge and growth. This journey is a lifelong learning process, and you need to continually follow the quest for knowledge to avoid sinking into yourself and becoming reclusive.

Seven as a Soul Number

When you have seven as a soul number, a major lesson in your life is learning how to balance your need for solitude and self-discovery with being an active member of society. For you, the perfect place would be a serene, isolated island, where it could just be you and your thoughts, plus a new exotic landscape to explore and satisfy your inquisitive nature. For you, a little isolation is necessary, and while you recognize that you can't just disappear somewhere by yourself forever, it can be difficult for you to know when to come back and join the rest of us.

With your natural inclination to academics and higher knowledge, you might be perceived as introverted and untouchable. This is a false judgment, but you understand this because there have been plenty of times that you have also judged on the basis of superficial knowledge. The real you is one that is warm and intimate. You only allow certain people into your life, but when you do, you make a great effort to really understand them. This is how you, as a seven, can differentiate between people you genuinely care for and people who are temporary fillers in your personal life. If you are genuinely interested in the person, in their problems, in learning what makes them tick, then they are your people, part of your tribe. If you feel aloof, uninterested in the details of their life and find yourself being cynical towards them, then you know that this is not someone who will be with you in the long term. As a seven, you have the personal responsibility to cut off relationships with people to whom you do not feel connected, because once you start to turn away from someone, you have a tendency to be mean and harsh if they try to hang on.

Seven as a Personality Number

Seven is a curious cat. They are constantly poking around, sniffing about, and the whole time being so stealthy about it that you hardly even know that they are there. If you have seven as a personality number, chances are that you like to hang out in the back of the group, maybe even lurk in the shadows, because these positions give you the perfect opportunity to observe.

Sevens live in a world of depth. Their curiosity is deep, and their thoughts even deeper. Sevens do not have an appreciation for anything that is shallow, and that includes people who are untruthful and manipulative.

While seven has a dry, almost sarcastic sense of humor, they know how to see the humor around them and find irony funny. Not everyone catches on to the personality of seven, but that is OK, because honestly, the seven is one of the pickiest numbers when it comes to choosing their inner circle. Once you are in, however, the seven is warm, generous and loyal. If you have someone with the personality number seven in your life, you will likely find yourself needing to gently nudge them back in from their thoughts. No need to worry, though; they will have incredible stories to tell you about where they just were.

Eight

Key Words and Traits: Success, Achievement, Problem Solver, Power, Gain

When you first look at the number eight, you might notice one of several things, each of them very different. The number eight is associated with business and power, so naturally, many people see a similarity between the 8 and the dollar symbol. When we look at the number, we can also see that the top and the bottom are balanced. There is a harmony here that is inherent in the very structure of the number. Finally, the number eight also has a similar shape to the infinity symbol, with its unending, recycling energy. To get the best overall picture of the energy associated with the number eight, we need to combine all of these images together.

First, we can address the power aspect of the number eight. Of all the numbers, eight is the one most closely connected with power, authority and material belongings. However, the energy of the number is not as hard and cold as that description illustrates. The eight is balanced, and when it is present in your life, you can guarantee that balance will exist, whether it feels like it is working for or against you. The eight will not let you reap the rewards if you have not put in the hard work. It will also protect you from falling toward negative energies, because it will always be at work, pulling you back to an equilibrium.

The energy of the number eight is straightforward. It recognizes what needs to be done and uses all its attributes to accomplish the goal. If you are looking to appeal to the softer side of an eight, you need to do it through logic rather than emotion. To an eight, reacting to or with emotion is impractical. It is not that the eight is completely heartless; it is that they know that it is difficult to act in the most efficient and productive way when you are influenced by emotional pulls.

Trouble arises for the number eight when it does not pay attention to its need for balance. Someone with many eights in their chart might be an overachiever, with success being their main goal. With this mindset, it can be difficult not to lose sight of all the other energy aspects of the number. When the eight is balanced, success is assured. When the eight lets its focus become too narrow, it often falls far and hard.

Positive Traits of Number Eight Energy
- Forward Thinking
- Goal Oriented
- Successful
- Hardworking
- Overachieving

Negative Traits of Number Eight Energy
- Shallow
- Materialistic
- Controlling
- Greedy
- Self-Centered

Eight as a Life Path Number

With eight as a life path number, you likely have a long to-do list that you carry around, but checking items off of it is almost effortless for you. Oftentimes, the presence of your energy alone is enough to get things done. The words "fail" and "not possible" are not in your vocabulary, and your confidence is contagious. With eight as your life path number, achievement and success come easy to you, and others will be attracted to this energy.

For you, this life path is not only about basking in the glow of your achievements, but also about learning how to be humble and recognizing the value in the opinions of others. Because you are familiar with success, sometimes you forget that you don't always have all the answers. You also tend to have a stubborn streak that can cause friction for you along the way if you don't make the effort to learn the fine art of compromise. In fact, you may find that you come up against the same obstacles repeatedly until you are able to appreciate the value of negotiation, compromise and equality.

Eight as a Destiny Number

With eight as a destiny number, you will often feel the pull of the separate but equal energies of the positive and negative sides of success. On one hand, your life seems charmed, and in many ways, it is. You are success-driven, intelligent, and you make hard work look so easy that others may not recognize your full effort. You set your sights on what you want, and in one way or another, it will be yours. The other side of this, remembering that the eight has two equal, opposite parts, is that you will have occasional struggles and setbacks. Unfortunately, if you are not prepared, these can be quite devastating.

Just as the eight has high points, it also has low points. For the eight it can feel like the universe is either offering up everything or nothing at all. While practically every successful company has eights among its top rungs of employees, you will also find more eights struggling financially than other numbers. Sometimes this is because the eight has the tendency to overthink things to the point of their own self destruction; it can also come from other people in the form of envy and jealousy. The key here is to be aware of these forces so that they don't catch you off guard and knock you down.

A good way to do this is for the eight to learn that success does not need to include praise or monetary gain (although when you are balanced you will find that people respect and value your skills and money woes won't be at the forefront of your worries). A good place for an eight to focus their energy is building other people up. Rather than focusing solely on your success, make a goal of focusing on the success of others as well.

Eight as a Soul Number

There is a softer side to the number eight that few people get the chance to see, mostly because the first thing that one notices about an eight is their success and confidence, which doesn't always equate easily with warm and intimate. The eight can seem a bit cold, or maybe even awkward, but even the steeliest boss with unreasonable expectations has a quieter, softer side that only a few people are allowed to see. With an eight as a soul number, a challenge for you is learning how to expose this to more people in a way that doesn't make you feel too vulnerable.

As an eight, you need to make an effort to open up your heart and realize that sometimes it is acceptable to let emotion take over in place of logic. It is OK to be romantic rather than practical, compromising rather than stern.

What the eight as soul number strives for is recognition. You are capable of achieving great things, and all that you ask is that people know it was you. You want to be remembered for your greatness. While this praise is well deserved, it is important for the soul number eight to remember that they are not alone in the world. Their success and their failures are influenced by other people, even if in ways so subtle that they go unnoticed. Keep yourself open to the idea that you are not alone, but a part of the greater whole. You are an important piece, but not the only piece.

Eight as a Personality Number

When the number eight shows up as your personality number, it is a sure sign that you are going to learn the lessons of balance and karma in this incarnation. You have an unyielding drive and like to be in control. Harness these energies in a way that helps you control the direction of your life path in a positive way, and those lessons learned will be much gentler.

As an eight, you have two sides to your personality. One side is so caught up in forward motion that you don't even notice what is going on around you, and the other side wants recognition for your hard work, which can manifest itself in materialism and greed. These can be struggles for you, especially in your youth, before maturity has a chance to step in and mellow some of your more materialistic and narrow focused tendencies.

Use caution when choosing your inner circle. Your success and drive mean that others want to be like you, and the best way to do that is by getting close to you. This is a great opportunity for you to serve as a positive role model for those who are genuinely interested in improving their lives, but be wary of those who may have malicious intent fueled by jealousy. Yours is an energy that is so sought-after that some people change their names, or try to manipulate their charts, so that they have stronger eight energy. As an eight, you have a beautiful soul. It is when you allow it to become tainted by the negative energy of others and superficial emotions that you run into trouble.

Nine

Key Words and Traits: Connection, Purity, Compassion, Nurturing, Completion

Finally, we arrive at nine, the last of the main single-digit numbers. This is a good time to look back at the number one, and over each of the numbers along the journey to this point. In essence, the number nine is the completion of the cycle, and in many ways, it is the exact opposite of the number one. However, it is also interesting to note that as a cycle completes, it becomes ready to begin again. In order for that to happen, the finishing point needs to share some characteristics with the starting point, so that the two blend seamlessly. Nine is the only number that can accomplish all of this.

Nine is the number of connection. We can take a look back at the number six and reflect on its maternal energy. Nine is physically very much the same as six, except it is upside down. However, this doesn't reverse the energy of the number six; instead, it amplifies it. Where six was the nurturer and loving caregiver to those closest to her, nine is the nurturer and healer of the world. Nine acts on a large scale, and has the strongest energy of connection.

There is a great deal of purity associated with the number nine. When this number is strong in a chart, you can be assured that there is pure intent, pure compassion and pure power. When a nine walks the earth, you can almost feel the energy part in its path. As the nine will be the first to offer its hand to you, it will also be the first to use its power against you if it feels you have been unjust. Nine is the great equalizer and holds everyone to the same standards.

The nine can be difficult to understand and guarded in matters of the heart. It is serious business feeling this nurturing to everyone. When you let someone in, they are able to see your weak spots and your vulnerabilities, and nines have no interest in exposing themselves this way. Despite their generous and nurturing spirit, nines can seem distant and cold.

If you have strong nines in your chart, now is a time of completion. You are coming to an end of a cycle in your life. For some people, this will come in the form of great changes, while for others it will present itself as a time for rest before beginning anew. Either way, the nine has incredible energy, and this incarnation will be an interesting one.

Positive Traits of Number Nine Energy
- Calm
- Honest
- Compassionate
- Dependable
- Accepting

Negative Traits of Number Nine Energy
- Distant
- Cold
- Inscrutable
- Tactless
- Overburdened

Nine as a Life Path Number

There is a gentleness that surrounds an incarnation with a life path number of nine. You are like a calm reprieve in a violent storm. You emit a certain energy that makes others feel as though everything is going to be OK. You are a pillar of strength and dependability. You have not only learned the lessons, but also know how to apply them in life. You think before you act, and you act with the greater good in mind.

One of the most beautiful aspects of the number nine is its complete inability to place judgment. If nine is your life path number, you accept things at face value. You know that this type of acceptance is the only way to bring about change. This same energy makes you a very honest person, to the point that others might view your honesty as a little harsh. Your type of nurturing doesn't involve just wiping away the tears, but helping a person look at themselves honestly in the mirror. You will be faced with opposition from those not ready for this level of honesty, and you may be challenged to expose more of your vulnerable side in the process.

When you think of an end to a cycle, ask yourself what things are important for completion. Honesty, forgiveness, and acceptance top the list. These are important qualities that will remain strong throughout your entire incarnation as a nine.

Nine as a Destiny Number

The destiny number nine is as much of a doer as the eight is; however, it is more concerned about success on a global scale rather than just on a personal level. The nine is looking for completion and wants a positive outcome. It will not let anything stand in the way of this happening. As we get to these higher numbers, such as eight and nine, you notice an increased drive and focus. This is similar to the energy you might have for a work project as the deadline approaches. You have had time to plan, strategize, reflect and practice. Now, it is time to get to work before the opportunity is forever gone. This is the driving force behind the nine's need to create change.

Nine is intuitive and empathetic. You will find plenty of nines participating in humanitarian activities. Nines do not need praise or reward for their good deeds, although it is always appreciated when you do recognize them.

With nine as your destiny number, there will periods of your life devoted to serving others, but not so much in the self-sacrificing way of some of the other numbers. For you, this is about karma and balance. You already know that self-neglect is counterproductive.

Nine as a Soul Number

If there is one thing that plagues a person with the soul number of nine, it is that it is impossible to solve all the problems at once. Most of the time a nine knows its limits, but there will be occasions when it simply bites off more than it can chew. To a nine, we all share the same world, and we all have the same obligation to make it a good place. There is so much heartache, disease, and stress that it is almost unavoidable to feel overburdened at some point. Not to worry, though; the nine will bounce back.

With a soul number of nine, you have a genuine spirit. Some might find it hard to believe that there are people in this world who are as committed to the greater good as you are. You might find that people around you are suspicious. My advice is to ignore them. After all, they have their own journey that they are undertaking, and learning how to see the purity of intentions in other people might be part of their own process. For you, following career and hobby paths that lead you in the direction of service will be most rewarding. Find your cause and focus in on it. You can't make the world a better place in one large step; it takes many small ones. This is a lesson that you will continue to work on during this incarnation.

Nine as a Personality Number

If you have nine as a personality number, you like to make change without making waves. You are a gentle soul, but also a mature one. You know when to charge forward and when to hold back. You know when to intervene and when to let things unfold naturally. You value success, but not in monetary terms. You are quiet and contemplative, but firm and assertive when necessary. You place a high value on morals and expect those closest to you to do the same.

As a nine, the energies of love, acceptance and rationality are your driving forces. You are compassionate, yet realistic. You help others recognize and reach their potential, but will not tolerate excuses and untruths. You have come full circle in so many ways, and now that knowledge is yours to share with others. Do not waste this opportunity by second guessing yourself. Do not let the negativity of others hold you back. It is rare that a nine succumbs to these types of energies; however, we all have moments of weakness and uncertainty, and these are vulnerable spots for the otherwise strong nine.

In this incarnation, do what brings you pleasure, which is most likely something that benefits the greater good. Those around you need to see that it is possible to give to others while remaining balanced. This life is one of service, but not the kind that burdens you in any way. This is the life where you finally have the chance to share all your gifts with the world.

The Masters: 11, 22 and 33

In numerology, all numbers are significant, with their own unique energies. However, there are three numbers that are especially significant and powerful. These are the numbers eleven, twenty-two and thirty-three, and we refer to them as the master numbers.

When we look at numbers in numerology, we generally want to reduce them down until we find a single-digit number that is symbolic of the larger number. However, there are times that this doesn't apply, such as in the case of karmic debt numbers and master numbers. When these numbers appear, we either don't reduce them down any further, or we stop and take note of the significance and energy of the number before reducing it further. Master numbers have an increased vibration, and people with master numbers in their charts have special gifts and challenges. Understanding these two sides of energy for each master number is important, especially if you see them repeatedly in yours or someone else's chart. The more a master number appears, the stronger its influence in that person's life.

Some belief systems in numerology take each duplicate double-digit number (44, 55, 66, etc.) as a master number. While these numbers can be more powerful than their single-digit counterparts, they do not hold the same significance in terms of energy as eleven, twenty-two and thirty-three. Also, the higher you go with duplicate double digits, the less likely you are to encounter them in a numerology chart. The master numbers that we describe here are different. First, you can take the energy of each of the digits and multiply by two. For example, if someone has the number thirty-three in their chart, they have the energy of the number three, times two. Furthermore, the master numbers consist of two numbers that you can add together, and you will also exhibit the energy of that sum. For example, the master number 11 has two ones. Once you understand the masculine energy of the number one, you can easily see the powerful energy behind this number. Now, if you break eleven down into 1+1, you get a two, which in terms of energy is the exact opposite of the number one. On one hand, this will help balance the one energy, but on the other hand it can result in difficulties and conflict, both internal and external. Let's take a closer look at each of the master numbers and their energies.

Eleven

Each master number has an underlying theme. In the case of eleven, that theme is enlightenment and universal connection. Most people with the number eleven in their chart are attracted to spirituality and metaphysics. For them, this isn't just a curiosity, but an inner drive. They are fueled by learning and connecting to the mysterious. The number eleven is also highly tuned into subtle vibrations. People who are psychic, or have a highly developed sense of intuition, often have elevens in their charts.

Eleven believes in the connection between the physical and spiritual worlds, and understanding and respecting that connection is important to them. Because they are so sensitive to these subtle energies, they can also pick up on even the smallest undercurrents in the physical world. Number eleven often makes a great counselor for this reason. They just intuitively know what is going on. However, the eleven still has a long way to go in terms of development, and their energy can be flighty and unbalanced. Their intense curiosity for the spiritual world may leave them a little ungrounded in the physical world.

To understand the positive and negative traits of the master number eleven, all you need to do is look at the two primary numbers involved, which are one and two. The free, flowing and inquisitive nature of eleven can be connected to the feminine energy of the number two, while the direct line of approach is definitely related to the number one. When in harmony and balanced, the number eleven is spiritual, gifted, honest, straightforward, objective and fair. When unbalanced, the number eleven is moody, dark, cynical, unyielding, cold and harsh.

Twenty -Two

The master number twenty-two is one of double feminine energy. Where the eleven is on a spiritual quest for personal knowledge, the twenty-two takes this knowledge and applies it to the life around her. The twenty-two takes dreams and makes them a reality. She is a master builder. There is an energy of transformation within the twenty-two. She can take something that is ethereal and make it concrete. She, in her own way, is able to materialize the connection between the spiritual world and the physical world. The twenty-two completes her journey by being pragmatic, practical and ambitious while still maintaining her connection to the subtle energies around her.

On the darker side of twenty-two lurks an equally strong destructive energy. The twenty-two is so pragmatic, so structured, that opposition can throw it off guard. Too many distractions or obstacles will cause the twenty-two to cave inward, sometimes to the point of self-destruction. The twenty-two also needs to be fueled. This might be by a mentor, academics or spiritual inspiration. When that fuel is not provided, or sought after, the twenty-two can lose sight of its personal power and completely miss the opportunity to reach its full, glorious potential.

Thirty-Three

When we speak in terms of energy, twenty-two radiates the strongest, but when we speak in terms of true mastery, it is the number thirty-three that steps up to the plate. When we add the other two master numbers, eleven and twenty-two, we end up with the sum of thirty-three. Thirty-three is the number of mastery, completion and self-realization.

When a person has the number thirty-three in their chart, you can count on them being knowledgeable and seeming wise beyond their years. They have experienced the deep spiritual seeking of the number eleven and the dedicated servitude and creation of the number twenty-two. Thirty-three has completed all the phases of growth and now is here to help humanity with its knowledge and enlightenment. If you have the number thirty-three in your chart, you have a great deal to share with the world.

In some numerology systems, you will not see the number thirty-three listed at all. This is because it is said to hold energy only when it shows up as a core number (life path, destiny, soul, or personality number). There are no months with thirty-three days, so you will not find thirty-three as a personal day number. This master number is not said to hold much significance or power in other realms, but I believe that its energy should be acknowledged any time that it shows up in your chart.

Living Consciously Through Numerology

The art and science of numerology is based on the symbolism and vibrational energy of numbers. Numbers are everywhere in our lives, from the rhythmic beat of a heart, to the miraculous numerical arrangement of leaves and petals in nature, to the fact that science depends upon numbers to uncover the reason for our very existence. Numbers surround us and are within us every second of every day. The universe itself is a myriad of numerical vibrations.

Some are quick to dismiss the power of numerology, claiming that it is a mystical art with no real substance. To those naysayers, I would like to ask them to strip away the mysticism of numerology for just a moment and look at the fact that it is through numbers that we are able to understand and grasp the world around us. Where would we be if it weren't for numbers? Even the most skeptical are quick to acknowledge that they might consider a certain number lucky or unlucky, or perhaps subscribe to certain superstitions centered around numbers. We can take this further and look at the basic structure of the family. The number of siblings in a family can greatly alter its energy, and personality traits associated with birth order are commonly acknowledged. These are all ways that the subtle energy of numbers affects us—even those of us who resist the idea that numerology can have an impact on our lives.

Once you acknowledge the energetic power behind each number, and once you learn how these subtle energies can have a major impact in your life and the lives of others, you are then given a certain responsibility. This is a personal responsibility that lies in your potential to strive for personal and spiritual growth. It involves a personal responsibility to acknowledge your place in this life and the gifts that you have to share with others. It also comes with the responsibility to recognize and acknowledge your areas of potential growth. Once you understand the significance of numerology, you gain clarity and insight into the world around you and the needs and nature of mankind. You begin to understand how we all work together, even when it seems as though we are at odds. Every one of us, with each of our individual struggles and challenges, resonates with a limited range of numbers. This means that in the end, we all have much more in common than we have separating us.

With numerology, there is the potential to access the highest level of human spiritual development. Through numerology, we learn how to become compassionate and empathetic, and how to think outside of ourselves. Numerology provides a vision of the big picture. Suddenly, you understand that destiny exists, and that you chose this life. Your struggles, your achievements, are all yours to claim. There is great power in this acknowledgement of personal responsibility. When you realize that your soul, working at a higher level of consciousness, chose the date that you were to enter this life, and the energy that would be carried with you from that date and the name that you chose to be born with, the obstacles that once seemed insurmountable begin to make sense. The lessons that you just didn't understand begin to fall into place, and with this you also gain a greater appreciation for all the people, things and circumstances of your life that you are grateful for. Numerology is empowerment on every level.

As numerology provides the tools to connect the past and the present, it also provides everything that you need to prepare for a better future. Numerology is understanding that there is power in the "now," and that everything that came before this, and everything that will come in the future, is interconnected. Numerology helps us better understand our purpose, our gifts and our challenges. You are a being with unlimited potential, and numerology is a tool that can help you discover and unlock this potential so that you may live your most beautiful, empowering life.

Also by Clarissa Lightheart

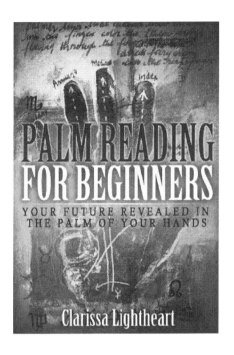

Made in the USA
San Bernardino, CA
16 July 2020

75573493R00080